Scientific and Engineering Computation
Janusz Kowalik, editor

A Programmer's Guide to ZPL

Lawrence Snyder

The MIT Press
Cambridge, Massachusetts
London, England

This book was set in Times Roman by Wellington Graphics and was printed and bound in the United States of America.

Library of Congress Cataloging-in-Publication Data

Snyder, Lawrence.
  A programmer's guide to ZPL / Lawrence Snyder.
    p.   cm. — (Scientific and engineering computation)
  Includes bibliographical references and index.
  ISBN 0-262-69217-1 (pbk.: alk. paper)
  1. ZPL (Computer program language) I. Title. II. Series.
QA76.73.Z27S69   1999
502.85′51—dc21   98-34702
                                                                                     CIP

Dedicated to the memory of A. Nico Habermann
and the many delightful hours spent discussing
programming language design and compiler construction.

Contents

The world of modern computing potentially offers many helpful methods and tools to scientists and engineers, but the fast pace of change in computer hardware, software, and algorithms often makes practical use of the newest computing technology difficult. The Scientific and Engineering Computation series focuses on rapid advances in computing technologies and attempts to facilitate transferring these technologies to applications in science and engineering. It will include books on theories, methods, and original applications in such areas as parallelism, large-scale simulations, time-critical computing, computer-aided design and engineering, use of computers in manufacturing, visualization of scientific data, and human-machine interface technology.

The series will help scientists and engineers to understand the current world of advanced computation and to anticipate future developments that will impact their computing environments and open up new capabilities and modes of computation.

Janusz S. Kowalik

This guide seeks to be a complete primer to the ZPL programming language and the programming style that it introduces. The presentation assumes the reader is experienced with an imperative programming language such as C, Fortran, Pascal, Ada, and the like. Though precise and in most instances thorough, the guide does not attempt to be a reference manual for ZPL. Rather, it illustrates typical ZPL usage and explains in an intuitive way how the constructs work. Emphasis is placed on teaching the reader to be a ZPL programmer. Scientific computations are used as examples throughout.

A compiler, libraries, and complete information about ZPL are located at the ZPL home page at `http://www.cs.washington.edu/research/zpl/`.

Acknowledgments

ZPL is the product of many people's ideas and hard work. It is a pleasure to thank Calvin Lin with whom the initial structure of the language was designed. Calvin has led a committed and enthusiastic team of implementors of the prototype ZPL system: Brad Chamberlain, Sung-Eun Choi, E. Chris Lewis, Jason Secosky, and Derrick Weathersby, with contributions at the early stages from Ruth Anderson, George Forman, and Kurt Partridge. These dedicated computer scientists have devoted their minds and hearts to the realization of ZPL's goals. It is a pleasure to acknowledge their creativity: they have given life to ZPL. Others have offered thoughtful input and comment on the language, including A. J. Bernheim, Jan Cuny, Marios Dikaiakos, John G. Lewis, Ton Ngo, and Peter Van Vleet.

This document has undergone numerous revisions, and many people have contributed suggestions for its improvement. Thanks are due to George Turkiyahh for his input on the N-body computation, Sung-Eun Choi for her comments on median finding and her contributions with Melanie Fulgham to random numbers, Victor Moore for suggesting vector quantization, Martin Tompa for assisting with global alignment, and Brad Chamberlain for his input on the presentation of advanced topics. E. Lewis and Sung-Eun Choi pointed out numerous improvements to the programs and text. Finally, it is a pleasure to thank the ever-helpful Judy Watson.

The ZPL research has been supported in part by Office of Naval Research grant N00014-89-J-1368, the Defense Advanced Research Projects Agency under grants N00014-92-J-1824 and E30602-97-1-0152, and the National Science Foundation grant CCR 97-10284.

A Programmer's Guide to ZPL

1 Introduction

ZPL is a new programming language that is especially effective for scientific and engineering computations. It is intended to replace languages such as Fortran and C for technical computing. The programming advantages of ZPL will become evident as its features are explained in subsequent chapters. In this chapter ZPL is illustrated to give the curious a quick overview, and to prepare the student for the more thorough presentation to follow.

What Is ZPL?

ZPL* is a programming language suitable for scientific and engineering computations. It can be described in other ways as well:

· ZPL is an *array language*. Expressions such as X + Y have been generalized to apply to whole arrays as well as simple scalars, depending on how X and Y are declared. The language has standard programming constructs, such as if statements and procedures. These concepts have their normal meaning, though there is often an array generalization. Expressions involving arrays are convenient and natural to write, especially for scientists and engineers. Not only does an array language save the programmer from writing many tedious loops and specifying error prone index calculations, it enables the compiler to identify parallelism that will speed the computation.

· ZPL is a *machine independent* programming language, meaning that ZPL programs run *well* on both sequential and parallel computers. Programmers need not concern themselves with machine specifics. Machine independence is an essential requirement for programs that will be shared among many researchers with different computers. It is probably most important for programs used over a long period of time, since they are simply recompiled when an old machine is replaced by a new one. Details of ZPL's most important machine independence feature, the what-you-see-is-what-you-get (WYSIWYG) performance capability, are presented in chapter 8.

ZPL is an *implicitly parallel* programming language. That is, although ZPL was designed to simplify programming parallel computers, programmers do not specify how the computation is performed concurrently. Nor do they insert interprocessor communication. The ZPL compiler is responsible for producing parallel object code from the source program, and for taking care of all details necessary to exploit the target parallel computer. There are times when the programmer will want to consider how the computation is performed in parallel, e.g., when deciding among alternative ways of implementing a computation.

* ZPL is mnemonic for the phrase "Z-level Programming Language," a reference to a component of the programming model that it implements [Alverson et al., 98].

But generally, programmers are only concerned with expressing the computation to produce the right result.

Perhaps the most important property of ZPL for scientific programmers is that it can be compiled to run fast on parallel computers. For example, the *Jacobi iteration,* which will be used as an example throughout the remainder of this chapter, has been reported to have the performance approximating C, as illustrated in figure 1.1 [Lin & Snyder 94]. In the experiment the program (illustrated in figure 1.2) was compiled, and then run on the Kendall Square Research KSR-2, a "shared memory" parallel computer, and the Intel Corporation Paragon, a distributed memory or "message passing" parallel computer. The two machines are representative of the principal classes of commercially available parallel computers. The program was executed until convergence (929 iterations). Its performance was compared with a C program handcoded for each machine.

The Jacobi computation is a simple program, and good performance is to be expected. Comparable results for other, more substantial computations have also been reported [Lin et al. 95, Ngo et al. 97].

Preliminary ZPL Concepts

Most ZPL concepts are intuitive and easy to understand by scientists and engineers familiar with other programming languages, e.g., Fortran or C. To introduce these

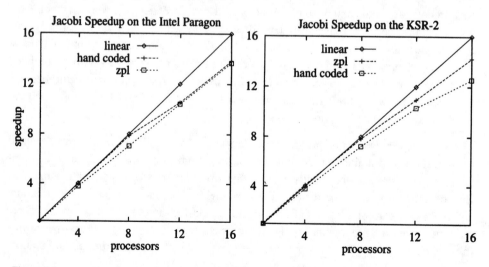

Figure 1.1
Speedup with respect to the handcoded C program for the Jacobi program executed on the Intel Paragon and the KSR-2

```
 1    program Jacobi;
 2    /*                 Jacobi Iteration
 3                       Written by L. Snyder, May 1994        */
 4    config var    n     : integer   = 512; -- Declarations
 5                  delta : float     = 0.000001;
 6
 7    region        R = [1..n, 1..n];
 8    var           A, Temp: [R] float;
 9                  err     : float;
10
11    direction     north = [-1,  0];
12                  east  = [ 0,  1];
13                  west  = [ 0, -1];
14                  south = [ 1,  0];
15
16    procedure Jacobi();
17    begin
18      [R]             A := 0.0;                    -- Initialization
19      [north of R]    A := 0.0;
20      [east  of R]    A := 0.0;
21      [west  of R]    A := 0.0;
22      [south of R]    A := 1.0;
23
24      [R]             repeat                       -- Body
25                        Temp := (A@north + A@east
26                                 + A@west + A@south)/4.0;
27                        err  := max<< abs(A - Temp);
28                        A    := Temp;
29                      until err < delta;
30    end;
```

Figure 1.2
ZPL program for the Jacobi computation

concepts, consider the Jacobi iteration as an example that illustrates representative usage.

Jacobi: Given an array A, iteratively replace its elements with the average of their four nearest neighbors, until the largest change between two consecutive iterations is less than delta.

For the example, the array A will be an $n \times n$ two dimensional array initialized to zero, except for the southern boundary, which is set to the constant 1.0 in each position. The tolerance delta will be 0.000001. The ZPL Jacobi program is shown in figure 1.2.

Several features of the language are evident, even without any explanation of how the program works.

Like most languages, ZPL programs begin with declaration statements. All variables in ZPL programs must be declared. The computational part of the program has been further subdivided by the programmer into "initialization" and "body" sections. Though this division of activities is not required by the language, it is generally good practice to concentrate initialization into a block at the start of the program.

There are punctuation characteristics of ZPL that are also evident from the Jacobi program.

The assignment symbol in ZPL is := with no space between the two characters. Assignment has the same meaning as in other programming languages that simply use an equal sign, e.g. Fortran and C. Thus, the value computed on the right-hand side becomes the value of the name indicated on the left-hand side. The equal sign is also used in ZPL, but it serves two other roles. First, the = symbol is used to give values to names in cases where the values cannot be changed in the program. The declaration section illustrates multiple uses of = in this form (lines 7, 11–14). Second, the equal sign is used when testing for equality, as might be required in an if-statement. As a simple intuitive rule, := is used for changing values of variables, while = is used in cases where equality is the intended meaning.

Unlike Fortran, but like C, every statement in ZPL is terminated with a semicolon. This is true even if it appears that some other word or punctuation character might also serve to indicate statement termination. Since the end-of-line is not a statement terminator, long statements can easily be written across multiple lines without any continuation symbols, as in the two-line assignment to Temp (lines 25–26).

The one role reserved for end-of-line in ZPL is as a comment terminator. ZPL has two kinds of comments:

Any text between -- and the end of the line is a comment.

Any text between /* and the first following */ is a comment.

Thus, the -- symbol is typically used for short comments (line 18), while a /* */ pair is used for multiline commentary (lines 2–3).

A Quick Tour of the Jacobi Program

Though all of the programming constructs will be explained later, a brief "walk through" of the Jacobi program of figure 1.2 can serve as an introduction to ZPL and its approach to computation.

A fundamental concept in ZPL is the notion of a *region*. A region is simply a set of indices. For example, (line 7),

```
region R = [1..n, 1..n];
```

specifies the standard indices of an n × n array, i.e., the set of ordered pairs { (1,1) , (1,2) , . . . , (n,n) }. Regions can be used to declare arrays of a size corresponding to the index set. Thus, (line 8),

```
var     A, Temp: [R] float;
```

declares two n × n array variables, A and Temp, composed of floating point numbers with indices given by region R. The final variable declaration, (line 9),

```
err: float;
```

does not mention a region, and so err is declared to be a simple scalar floating point variable.

The program next declares a set of four directions. Directions are used to transform regions. They are vectors with as many elements as the region has dimensions. The four 2-dimensional direction declarations, (lines 11–14),

```
direction    north = [-1, 0];
             east  = [ 0, 1];
             west  = [ 0,-1];
             south = [ 1, 0];
```

point unit distance in the four cardinal compass directions. For example, north of any index position will be found by subtracting one from the first element of the index pair. Examples of transforming regions with directions include expressions with "of" and "@", illustrated momentarily.

Regions also allow ZPL computations to be extended to operate on entire arrays without explicit looping. By prefixing a statement with a region specifier, which is simply the region name in brackets, the operations of the statement are applied to all elements in the array. Thus, (line 18),

```
[R]   A := 0.0;
```

assigns 0.0 to all n^2 elements of array A.

Since many scientific problems have boundary conditions, it is often necessary to provide borders to array data structures. In Fortran or C this is accomplished by increasing the size of an array from, say, n × n to n+2 × n+2, but doing so misaligns the indices. In ZPL the region specifier can be used to augment arrays with borders. Extending the array A with borders and initializing their values is the role of the next four lines, (lines 19–22),

```
[north of R]   A := 0.0;
[east  of R]   A := 0.0;
```

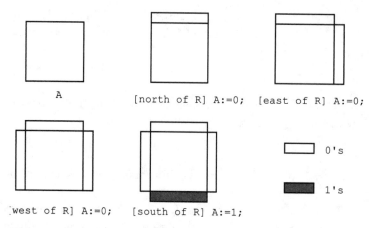

A

[north of R] A:=0;   [east of R] A:=0;

☐ 0's

■ 1's

west of R] A:=0;   [south of R] A:=1;

Figure 1.3
Schematic of the creation and initialization of borders of A

```
[west  of R]    A := 0.0;
[south of R]    A := 1.0;
```

The region specifier [d of R] is an expression that defines a region adjacent to R in the d direction, i.e., above R for the case where d = north. The statement is then applied to the elements of the region. Thus, [north of R] defines the index set which is a 0th row for A. Since A does not have these indices, the ZPL compiler extends A to have a 0th row. The assignment A := 0.0 initializes these elements with 0.0. The successive effects of the four initialization statements are illustrated in figure 1.3. (The programmer could include the "missing" corner elements simply by using a direction pointing towards the corner, e.g., [northeast of R].)

With the declarations and initialization completed, programming the computation is simple. The repeat-loop, which iterates until the condition becomes true, has three statements:

· Compute a new approximation by averaging all elements (lines 25–26).

· Determine the largest amount of change between this and the new iteration (line 27).

· Update A with the new iteration (line 28).

Since the repeat statement is prefixed by the [R] region specifier, all statements in the loop are executed in the context of the R region, i.e., over the indices of R. The statements operate as follows.

The averaging illustrates how explicit array indexing is avoided in ZPL by referring to adjacent array elements using the @ operator with a direction. The statement, (lines 25–26),

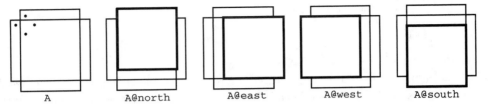

Figure 1.4
Referencing A modified by @ in the context of a region specifier covering all of A; the dots shown in A correspond to element (1,1) in the shifted arrays

```
Temp := (A@north + A@east + A@west + A@south) / 4.0;
```

finds for each element in A the average of its four nearest neighbors and assigns the result to Temp. An expression A@d, executed in the context of a region R, results in an array of the same size and shape as R offset in the direction d, and composed of elements of A. As illustrated in figure 1.4, A@d can be thought of as adding d to each index, or equivalently in this case, shifting A.

Since the region specifier on the repeat-loop provides the context for all statements in the loop body, the operations of this statement are applied to all elements of the arrays. The four arrays are combined elementwise, yielding the effect of computing for element (i, j) the sum of its four nearest neighbors. This can be seen by the following identities:

$(i, j)@north \equiv (i, j) + north \equiv (i, j) + (-1, 0) \equiv (i-1, j)$
$(i, j)@east \equiv (i, j) + east \equiv (i, j) + (0, 1) \equiv (i, j+1)$
$(i, j)@west \equiv (i, j) + west \equiv (i, j) + (0, -1) \equiv (i, j-1)$
$(i, j)@south \equiv (i, j) + south \equiv (i, j) + (1, 0) \equiv (i+1, j)$

Each of the n^2 sums is then divided by 4.0 and the result is stored into Temp.

To compute the largest change of any element between the current and the next iteration, (line 27), more elementwise array operations are performed. The underlined subexpression,

```
err := max<< abs(A - Temp);
```

causes the elements of Temp to be subtracted from the corresponding elements of A, and then the (floating point) absolute value of each element is found yielding an intermediate array with values abs($A_{1,1}$-$Temp_{1,1}$), abs($A_{1,2}$-$Temp_{1,2}$), ..., abs($A_{n,n}$-$Temp_{n,n}$). This computes the magnitude of change of all the elements. To find the largest among these, a maximum reduction (max<<) is performed. This operation "reduces" the entire array to its largest element. The maximum is then assigned to err, a scalar variable, that controls the loop.

The final statement of the loop, (line 28),

```
A := Temp;
```

installs `Temp` as the updated value of A.

The termination test for the iteration, `err < delta`, is simply the comparison of two scalar values, since both are declared as scalars. The `delta` variable is a *configuration* parameter, meaning that it is given a default value in the declaration at the top of the program. Optionally, the value can be changed on the command line when the program is executed. Thus, both the size of the problem (n) and the tolerance, can be changed on successive runs without recompiling the program.

Learning ZPL from this Guide

It takes some time to learn any programming language. But programmers report that ZPL is very intuitive and has few idiosyncrasies, so it is regarded as easy to learn. This guide has been organized to aid in acquiring basic proficiency quickly:

• Chapter 2 describes those ZPL features found in other programming languages; most readers with programming experience should be able to read this chapter quickly.

• Chapter 3 explains the most fundamental concepts new to ZPL; nearly all of them have been introduced in this chapter.

• Chapter 4 illustrates these concepts with small programming examples.

At the completion of chapter 4, it should be possible to write and run simple ZPL programs. Although the computations may be trivial, it is advantageous to run a program just to become familiar with the mechanics of program compilation and execution.

• Chapter 5 introduces more powerful concepts, including global operations.

• Chapter 6 presents another batch of examples illustrating the new concepts.

• Chapter 7 completes the language introduction by presenting advanced concepts.

At the completion of chapter 5 more interesting programs can be written and run, and after chapter 7, essentially the full power of the language is available.

• Chapter 8 explains information programmers will want to know if they plan to run ZPL programs on parallel computers.

• Chapter 9 describes programming techniques with further examples.

Though these last chapters are optional in terms of getting started with the language, they may be the most important for programmers who want to produce high quality machine independent programs.

Acquiring ZPL Programming Technique

Like all programming languages, there is a certain technique to writing in ZPL. "Technique" refers to the basic programming idioms, the "standard" ways to encode data and operate on it, tricks and other experiential knowledge programmers use when they program. For example, Fortran programmers "know" to traverse an array down the columns, while C programmers "know" to traverse it across the rows, because the arrays are stored in that order, respectively, and so locality, and hence performance, are enhanced. Though this knowledge is part of the programming technique for these languages, it is not ZPL technique, since traversing an array is rare. In ZPL manipulating whole arrays is basic, and the compiler performs the traversing. This motivates developing a new programming technique.

When first writing ZPL code, a common pitfall is to rely too literally on known techniques. Programmers learning ZPL often think of computations in terms of the primitive scalar operations required in other programming languages, rather than the whole array manipulations those primitive operations implement. Consequently, when thinking about how to write a ZPL program, a common mistake of first-time programmers is to attempt to express these primitive scalar operations directly in ZPL. Though it is possible, it's the compiler's task to produce the primitive scalar code. The programmer's task is to express the high level array manipulations that define the computation.

For example, many of us know the dense matrix-matrix multiplication computation as a triply nested loop that is frequently shown in Fortran or C programming manuals,

```
FORTRAN MM

    DO 10 J = 1,N
      DO 10 I = 1,N
        DO 10 K = 1,N
10        C(I,J)=C(I,J)+A(I,K)*B(K,J)
```

```
C  MM

for (i=0;i<n;i++){
  for (j=0;j<n;j++){
    for (k=0;k<n;k++){
      c[i][j]=c[i][j]
        +a[i][k]*b[k][j];
    }
  }
}
```

This code describes one way to compute matrix product using element-at-a-time scalar operations, but it is not the definition of the computation taught in linear algebra class. There, students are told that $\mathbf{C}_{ij}$ is the dot-product of row i of $\mathbf{A}$ and column j of $\mathbf{B}$. This definition, if interpreted literally, does not lead to a very efficient computation, and so may be considered to be too abstract. The ZPL solution is intermediate, less abstract than linear algebra, but more abstract than an element-at-a-time approach.

As explained in chapter 6, the "obvious" ZPL program for matrix multiplication is

```
[1..n,1..n] for k := 1 to n do
               C +=  (>>[,k] A) * (>>[k,] B);
           end;
```

which replicates the kth column of A and the kth row of B to compute the kth term of all of the dot-products for C at once. (The necessary concepts are explained in chapter 5.) This approach may not be the first matrix multiplication solution to come to mind, but as ZPL technique is acquired, it is more likely to become natural. The statement has all the characteristics of good ZPL technique: It computes over arrays rather than scalars, in this case rows and columns; it uses the powerful flood operator (>>) to be space efficient; it is very efficient on parallel computers [van de Geijn & Watts 97]; and at three lines is about the shortest solution possible.

The conclusion is that programming in an array language requires a different technique than programming in a scalar language. This book gives numerous examples and illustrations to help the reader acquire good ZPL technique. Perhaps, at the start an array solution will take more thinking, but the thinking will involve high-level concepts, not the nitty-gritty details of subscript expressions. Once one acquires the technique, programming in ZPL is natural, and the solutions are likely to be shorter, easier to write, simpler to debug and elegant. An array language is just more convenient.

References

G. A. Alverson, W. G. Griswold, C. Lin and L. Snyder, 1998, "Abstractions for Portable, Scalable Parallel Programming," *IEEE Transactions on Parallel and Distributed Systems,* 9(1):71–86.

Calvin Lin & Lawrence Snyder, 1994, "SIMPLE Performance Results in ZPL," In K. Pingali, U. Banerjee, D. Gelernter, A. Nicolau and D. Padua (Eds.), *Languages and Compilers for Parallel Computing,* Springer-Verlag, pp. 361–375.

C. Lin, L. Snyder, R. E. Anderson, B. Chamberlain, S. Choi, G. H. Forman, E. C. Lewis, W. D. Weathersby, 1995, "ZPL vs HPF: A Comparison of Performance and Programming Style," Technical Report 95-11-05, University of Washington.

Ton A. Ngo, Lawrence Snyder, Bradford Chamberlain, 1997, "Portable performance of data parallel languages," Proceedings of *SC97: High Performance Networking and Computing.*

Robert van de Geijn and Jerrell Watts, 1997, "SUMMA: Scalable universal matrix multiplication algorithm," *Concurrency Practice and Experience,* 9(4):255–274

2 Standard Constructs

ZPL has many features found in other programming languages. In this chapter those ZPL facilities that are similar to structures in other languages are briefly described, since they are likely to be familiar to experienced programmers.

Data Types

Variables in ZPL can be declared to be any of the following primitive data types. The data sizes are machine dependent, though typical sizes are given.

Value Types

Signed	Unsigned	
	boolean	logical data, stored as a byte
	char	printable character, byte size
sbyte	ubyte	byte data
shortint	ushortint	half size integer
integer	uinteger	standard size integer (32 bits)
longint	ulongint	double size integer
float		single precision floating point
double		double precision floating point (64 bits)
quad		quadruple precision* floating point (128 bits)
complex		single precision complex number
dcomplex		double precision complex number
qcomplex		quadruple precision* complex number

The unsigned types corresponding to signed types have one more bit of precision, but no negative representation. The complex types are pairs of floating point numbers of the indicated precision representing the real and imaginary parts of a complex number. Two other types, file and string, are provided, but have applications limited chiefly to I/O. (Chapter 4 treats basic I/O.)

Derived Types

array	d-dimensional array of elements of like type
indexed array	d-dimensional array of elements of like type
record	user defined type composed of fields

* Not available on some computers, where it defaults to double.

"Arrays" are called "parallel arrays" when it is necessary to distinguish them from "indexed arrays." The semantic distinction is explained in chapter 5.

Region Types

region	index set, defining iteration and value spaces
direction	tuple of signed integers for defining array offsets

Variations on the region types allow for both multiregions and multidirections. Unlike other types, the region types are "not first class," meaning that they cannot be assigned or passed to or from a procedure.

Operators

ZPL has a standard set of operators that partition into the usual groups.

Arithmetic Operators

+	addition
−	subtraction
*	multiplication
/	division
∧	exponentiation
+	plus (unary), i.e., no-op
−	negation (unary)
%	modulus, i.e., a%b = a mod b

Relational Operators

=	equality
!=	inequality
<	less than
>	greater than
<=	less than or equal to
>=	greater than or equal to

Logical Operators

!	logical negation (unary)
&	logical and
|	logical or

Additionally, bitwise operations on integers and shifting the bits of an integer are supported through the use of value returning built-in functions,

Bitwise Built-in Functions

`bnot(a)`	bitwise negation of the bits of integer `a`
`band(a,b)`	bitwise and of corresponding bits of integers `a`, `b`
`bor(a,b)`	bitwise or of corresponding bits of integers `a`, `b`
`bxor(a,b)`	bitwise exclusive or of corresponding bits of integers `a`, `b`
`bsl(s,a)`	shift bits of integer `s` left `a` places, filling with 0's
`bsr(s,a)`	shift bits of integer `s` right `a` places, filling with 0's

For the purposes of the logical operators, any zero operand value is taken to be logical false, and any nonzero operand value is taken to be logical true. Further, in the results of logical expressions, false and true are represented as 0 and 1, and have type boolean.

Exponentiation is compiled in a special way. When the exponent is a small integer constant, i.e., 2, 3 or 4, the ZPL compiler produces efficient customized code based on multiplication. In all other cases, i.e., larger integer constants, floats, etc., the built-in function `pow()` is invoked. When the exponent is 0.5, it is more efficient to use the built-in function `sqrt()`.

In general the operators have the precedence given in table 2.1.

When a sequence of binary operators of equal precedence is used without parentheses, left associativity is assumed, i.e.,

$$a - b - c - d \equiv ((a - b) - c) - d$$

Operators can generally be used with operands of any type according to the following convention: Given the ordering on base types,

Table 2.1
Precedence of ZPL operators. Notice that reduce, etc. bind more tightly than all binary arithmetic operators.

`+ - !`	(unary)	Highest precedence, binds most tightly
`<< || >> ##`	(reduce, scan, flood, permute)	
`^`		
`* / %`		
`+ -`	(binary)	
`< > <= >= = !=`		
`& |`		Lowest precedence, weakest binding

```
boolean                 Lowest
sbyte
ubyte, char
shortint
ushortint
integer
uinteger
longint
ulongint
float     complex
double    dcomplex
quad      qcomplex      Highest
```

any expression combining two base types produces a result of the *higher* type, which will be a complex type if either operand is complex.

Conversion to a specific type can be achieved by a function of the form

to_*type*()

where the nonitalic characters must be given literally, and *type* is chosen from the numeric types. Thus, to_float(i) converts variable i to its floating point equivalent. All conversions follow the rules of C, so conversion of numbers from higher to lower types can have unpredictable results.

ANSI C Object Code

The ZPL compiler converts ZPL source text to ANSI C object code. The resulting C program is then compiled for the target computer using the native C compiler for that computer together with machine specific libraries. These two steps are combined in the invocation of zc under UNIX. Generally, the base data types and operators presented in the last two sections will have their semantics determined by the characteristics of C and the implementing hardware.

Consequences of this process include:

· The size of certain base data types (shortint, ushortint, etc.) is inherited from the native C compiler; quad is available only if supported by the target C compiler.

· All properties of floating point arithmetic are inherited from the native C and hardware implementation, and may not conform to the IEEE standard.

· The standard scientific functions are derived from the C library math.h.

· Scalar C procedures can be used in a ZPL program if prototyped in ZPL (see chapter 5) and incorporated into the compilation.

Consult the installation notes for your version of the compiler for further information.

Identifiers

Identifiers are used to name variables and other constituents of ZPL programs. In general, an identifier is any combination of lower and uppercase letters including underscore (_) and numerals that does not start with a numeral. ZPL is *case sensitive*, meaning that

```
aaa, aaA, aAa, aAA, Aaa, AaA, AAa, AAA
```

are all distinct identifiers. The keywords of the language, e.g., `if`, `for`, `integer`, etc. are prohibited as identifiers.

As a convention ZPL programmers capitalize the first letter of array variables and regions as an aid to reading the program. Since most features of the language apply equally to arrays as well as to simple scalar values, signifying the arrays with capitals calls attention to them. Since they have characteristics in the language that scalars do not possess—they are a source of parallelism, require regions specifiers, etc.—it is helpful to distinguish them at a glance from scalars. This book follows the capitals-for-arrays policy.

Assignment

As described in the introduction, the basic assignment operator is `:=`, but ZPL has extended assignment operators in the style of C.

Assignments

`:=`	assignment			
`+=`	plus-equal	`a += b`	`≡ a:= a+b`	
`-=`	minus-equal	`a -= b`	`≡ a:= a-b`	
`*=`	times-equal	`a *= b`	`≡ a:= a*b`	
`/=`	divide-equal	`a /= b`	`≡ a:= a/b`	
`%=`	mod-equal	`a %= b`	`≡ a:= a%b`	
`&=`	and-equal	`a &= b`	`≡ a:= a&b`	
`|=`	or-equal	`a |= b`	`≡ a:= a|b`	

Notice that all assignments are statements, i.e., ZPL has no expression assignments.

Control-flow Statements

The control-flow of a language describes the order of execution of the program's statements. Though ZPL is efficiently executed in parallel, it derives its concurrency by applying operations to arrays, not by the programmer specifying statement sequences to execute simultaneously. Thus, except for "shattered control flow" discussed in chapter 5, *ZPL statements are executed one at a time.*

ZPL uses familiar control structures found in sequential languages.

Control-flow Statements

if *lexpression*   then *statements*
{else *statements*} end;
if *lexpression*   then *statements*
{{elsif *lexpression* then *statements*}}
{else *statements*} end;
for var := *low* to *high* {by *step*} do *statements* end;
for var := *high* downto *low* {by *step*} do *statements* end;
while *lexpression* do *statements* end;
repeat *statements* until *lexpression*;
return {*expression*};   -- from a procedure
exit;   -- from the innermost loop
continue;   -- to the next loop iteration
halt;   -- terminate execution
begin *statements* end;   -- compound statement

The non-italicized text must be given literally. Items in braces {} are optional; items in double braces {{}} may be repeated zero or more times. Italicized items must be replaced by program text of the proper type: *var* is a variable; *lexpression* is a logical expression; *low, high* and *step* are numerical expressions; *statements* is any statement sequence where each statement is terminated by a semicolon.

The control-flow statements, though generally self-evident, exhibit some characteristics worth noticing. The terminator for *statements* list is:

Statement list following	Terminated by
then	else, elsif or end;
else	end;
do	end;
repeat	until
begin	end;

The `for`-loop iteration variable is increased by *step* or 1 (if *step* is not given) when the separator between *low* and *high* is `to`; it is decreased by *step* or 1 when the separator is `downto`. Thus, there is no need for negative *step* values. There is no `goto` statement in ZPL. Rather, it is possible to selectively execute statements (`if`), to iterate (`for`, `while`, `repeat`), to preempt iteration (`exit`), to skip to the next loop iteration (`continue`) and to terminate execution (`halt`). Statements can be grouped into a *compound statement* using a `begin end` pair. These control structures are sufficient to realize any sequence of statement executions, and are thought to lead to more easily understood and debugged programs compared with programs that rely heavily on `goto`'s for their control flow.

The principal difference between using `else if` and using `elsif` can be seen by noticing the number of `end`'s required to terminate a cascade of tests:

```
if ...                           if ...
   then ...                         then   ...
   else if ...                      elsif ...
           then ...                 then   ...
           else if ...              elsif ...
                   then ...         then   ...
                   else ...         else   ...
                   end;             end;
           end;
   end;
end;
```

That is, each use of `if` starts a new (nested) statement that must eventually be terminated by an `end`, while `elsif` "continues" the `if` in which it appears.

Finally, since leading blanks and tabs are ignored, indenting is available to improve the readability of a program. Indenting, commenting and inclusion of white-space is recommended, as it is thought to promote readability.

3 ZPL Array Concepts

In this chapter basic array constructs of ZPL are explained. Each topic is treated in a separate section. The goal is to provide a sufficiently complete understanding of the basic concepts to write simple ZPL programs. (See chapter 4.) More advanced concepts are treated in subsequent chapters. The topics are:

Regions

Region Declarations

Array Declarations

Region Specifiers

Directions

Direction Declarations

Using Directions with "of"

Using Directions with "@"

Comparison of "of" vs "@"

Borders

Array and Cartesian Coordinates for Directions

Promotion

Index1, Index2, . . .

Reduce and Scan

Familiarity with the overall concepts of ZPL, as introduced in the Jacobi program walk-through of chapter 1, is assumed.

Regions

ZPL programmers write few loops in their programs and perform a minimum of index manipulation. This makes ZPL programs shorter, presumably easier to write and read, and with a lowered chance of notational errors. More importantly, the compiler is able to produce highly optimized code that runs well on sequential as well as parallel computers. The "region" concept is critical to making these advantages possible.

A *region* is a set of indices of a fixed rank. That is, a rank r region is the Cartesian product of r dense integer sequences, the lower and upper limits of which are programmer specified. The lower and upper limits are separated by "double dots," these pairs are separated by commas, and the whole specification is enclosed in brackets. Thus, an example 2×2 region is

```
[1..2, 1..2]  =  {(1,1), (1,2), (2,1), (2,2)}
```

where the pairs in parentheses are the rank 2 indices of the region. Rank r indices have r positions in the index tuples, called *dimensions*.

The limits are programmer-specified, so they can be *0-origin,* as in the 2×2 region,

```
[0..1, 0..1]  =  {(0,0), (0,1), (1,0), (1,1)}
```

or they can start and end at any other integral value, including negative values. Thus,

```
[-1..1,-1..1,-1..1] = {(-1,-1,-1),  (-1,-1, 0),  (-1,-1, 1),
                       (-1, 0,-1),  (-1, 0, 0),  (-1, 0, 1),
                       (-1, 1,-1),  (-1, 1, 0),  (-1, 1, 1),
                       ( 0,-1,-1),  ( 0,-1, 0),  ( 0,-1, 1),
                       ( 0, 0,-1),  ( 0, 0, 0),  ( 0, 0, 1),
                       ( 0, 1,-1),  ( 0, 1, 0),  ( 0, 1, 1),
                       ( 1,-1,-1),  ( 1,-1, 0),  ( 1,-1, 1),
                       ( 1, 0,-1),  ( 1, 0, 0),  ( 1, 0, 1),
                       ( 1, 1,-1),  ( 1, 1, 0),  ( 1, 1, 1),}
```

is a region of the 27 lattice points adjacent to the origin in three space, including the origin, and

```
[-10..10] = {(-10),  (-9),  (-8),  (-7),  (-6),
             ( -5),  (-4),  (-3),  (-2),  (-1),
             (  0),  ( 1),  ( 2),  ( 3),  ( 4),
             (  5),  ( 6),  ( 7),  ( 8),  ( 9),  (10)}
```

is a one dimensional array with indices spanning the interval from -10 to 10. The general form of a region specification in ZPL is

$$[l_1.. u_1, l_2..u_2, \ldots , l_r..u_r]$$

where l_1, u_1, l_2, u_2, $\ldots$, l_r, u_r are required to be integers, possibly signed, given as explicit constants, declared constants or configuration variables (see below), such that $l_i \le u_i$. The terminology is:

l_i is called the *lower limit* of dimension i.

u_i is called the *upper limit* of dimension i.

r is called the *rank* of the region.

$(u_i - l_i+1)$ is called the *size* of the ith dimension.

Notice the ordering of the dimensions is from left to right, i.e., $l_1..u_1$ is the index range of the *first* dimension.

The region is the Cartesian product of the integer intervals

$$[l_1 . . u_1, l_2 . . u_2, . . . , l_r . . u_r]$$
$$= \{l_1, l_1+1, . . . , u_1\} \times \{l_2, l_2+1, . . . , u_2\} \times . . . \times \{l_r, l_r+1, . . . , u_r\}$$

It must be emphasized that a region is simply an index set. It is not an array.

Region Declarations

Since scientific and engineering computations often perform operations repeatedly over a set of indices, it is convenient to give regions names to simplify their frequent use. The region declaration assigns a name to a region. For example,

```
region W = [1..10, 1..n];   -- Declaration of a 10 x n region
```

defines a two dimensional region W with indices ranging from 1 through 10 in the first dimension and from 1 through n in the second dimension.

The general form of a region declaration is

```
region RName = [l₁..u₁, l₂..u₂, . . . , lᵣ..uᵣ];
```

where *RName* is a user selected identifier that names the region. See table 3.1 This association remains fixed. As with all identifiers, it is thought to be good style to select meaningful names for regions, though because of their usage patterns programmers tend to prefer short names. Regions are "not first class," and so they cannot be assigned, or passed to or returned from procedures. See also dynamic regions in chapter 5.

Array Declarations

As noted above regions are simply sets of indices; they are not arrays. Separate declarations are required to define array variables, with regions giving the indices. Specifically, arrays are declared like other variables, except they have a region specified in brackets following the colon. (This is a region specifier, as explain next.) For example,

```
var A, B, C : [R] double;
```

declares three arrays with the same rank and index set, which is given by R. Though it is typical to declare arrays over regions that have been given names, it is not necessary. So

```
var U, V, W : [1..n] ubyte;
```

is a legal declaration for three vectors of unsigned bytes, using an explicit region specification. It is somewhat better style to use named regions to declare arrays, since presumably the region has a meaning in the problem solution, e.g., "interior" of problem

Table 3.1
Examples of region declarations

Example	rank	lower limit dim 1	upper limit dim 1	size, dim 1
region V=[-10..10];	1	−10	10	21
region Board=[1..8,1..8];	2	1	8	8
region Rubix=[1..4,1..4,1..4];	3	1	4	4
region Symmetric=[-10..10,-n..n];	2	−10	10	21

domain, "odd elements," etc., and associating the variables with this meaning is generally clarifying. But the main advantage to using named regions in array declarations is that the arrays can have borders "automatically allocated" as described below.

Region Specifiers

Region specifiers are region names or region expressions in square brackets, e.g., [V]. Though region specifiers are used for declaring arrays as just explained, their most common use is as prefixes to statements. When prefixing a statement, a region specifier of rank r asserts that all operations on rank r arrays in the statement are to be performed for the indices specified by the region. For example, assuming X, Y and Z are arrays with the same rank as the region V, the statement

```
[V]        X := Y + Z;
```

specifies that the elements of Y having indices in V are to be added to the corresponding elements in Z, i.e., those with the same indices, and the results of these sums are to be stored in the corresponding elements of X. X, Y and Z must be declared to have at least the indices of V, though they can have other indices as well. Any elements of X with indices not in V are unchanged by the assignment.

For example, the declarations

```
region   V       = [1..5];
         Vpre    = [1..3];
var      X, Y, Z : [V] integer;
```

define two regions and establish X, Y and Z as five element arrays with indices given by V. Assuming initial values

```
Y ≡ 1, 3, 5, 7, 9        Z ≡ 8, 6, 4, 2, 0
```

then the region specifiers on the statements

```
[V]     X := Y + Z;        -- X becomes 9, 9, 9, 9, 9
[Vpre]  X := X / 3;        -- X becomes 3, 3, 3, 9, 9
```

produce the indicated values. The second statement modifies only the first three elements of X and leaves the last two elements unchanged because Vpre contains the indices, (1), (2) and (3), corresponding to the first three values of X, while its last two indices, (4) and (5), are not in Vpre.

In general, (parallel) arrays cannot be used in ZPL unless a region specifier defines the indices to be used for array operations. Arrays of rank r require an r-dimensional region specifier. However, the region specifier does not have to appear on the statement to apply to its arrays. Region specifiers are *scoped,* which means that the applicable region specifier either prefixes the statement, or it prefixes an "enclosing" statement. Thus, using the initial conditions from the previous paragraph, in

```
[V]     begin
            . . .
            X := Y + Z;        -- X becomes 9, 9, 9, 9, 9
[Vpre]  X := X / 3;        -- X becomes 3, 3, 3, 9, 9
            X := X - 1;        -- X becomes 2, 2, 2, 8, 8
            . . .
        end;
```

region specifier [V] defines the indices used for all 1 dimensional arrays in all statements within the begin-end, except for the statement where the Vpre region specifier appears on the statement and over-rides it. Use of a region specifier on a statement effectively shields arrays of that statement from any enclosing region specifiers for that rank. If a rank r array is in the scope of a rank r region specifier, it is the array's *applicable region.*

Since arrays of different ranks will frequently be used, it is possible to prefix statements with multiple region specifiers. If V and W are regions of different rank, V1 and V2 are arrays with the same rank as region V, and W1 and W2 are arrays with the same rank as region W, then

```
[V] [W] if dim = 1
            then V1 := 2*V2;     -- Use region V
            else W1 := 2*W2;     -- Use region W
        end;
```

has the same meaning as

```
if dim = 1
    then [V] V1 := 2*V2;
    else [W] W1 := 2*W2;
end;
```

assuming that the `dim` variable is a scalar. That is, the statement in the `then`-clause will use the `[V]` region specifier since in either case—whether prefixing the statement or prefixing an enclosing statement—the computation involving `V1` and `V2` is in its scope.

Finally, the region specifiers of statements can take a variety of forms, including dynamic regions, as described in chapter 5.

Directions

Directions are vector constants used in ZPL to refer to relative positions. They are the mechanism for uniformly modifying the indices of a region to implement transformations such as translation. They are used as operands for the "at," "in" and "of" operators. Recall that in the Jacobi program four directions were declared:

```
direction    north = [-1,  0];
             east  = [ 0,  1];
             west  = [ 0, -1];
             south = [ 1,  0];
```

These enabled the programmer to refer to the nearest neighbors of A as A@north, A@east, etc.

Direction Declarations

In general, directions are declared as follows:

```
direction    Dname = [d₁, d₂, . . . , dᵣ];
```

where `direction` is a required keyword, *Dname* is a programmer selected identifier, which is the name of the direction, the d_i are (signed) integer constants, called *offsets,* and r is the rank of the direction. Directions of rank r are only meaningful with arrays or regions of rank r.

In directions the sign of the offset applies in terms of array indices, rather than Cartesian coordinates. Thus, *a negative offset in a dimension refers to elements with lower index values in that dimension, while a positive offset refers to elements with higher indices.*

This allows a direction to be added to a region to translate the dimension limits in matrix coordinates. For example,

```
direction    north = [-1, 0];
```

refers to the position "above" in relative orientation in a two dimensional array. As explained below, terms like "above" will be relative to array coordinates, but this does not preclude a Cartesian interpretation.

Directions are "not first class" so, once declared, they cannot be changed, assigned to variables, or passed to or from procedures.

Using Directions with "of"

It is often convenient to define one region from another. The most common example is when a border is being defined for an array. The "of" operator uses a direction and a region to define a new region adjacent to a previously defined region. The general form is

```
[d of R]
```

where d is a direction and R is a region, called the *base* region. The semantics are to define a new set of indices relative to R. Let

```
R = [l1..u1, l2..u2, . . ., lr..ur]
```

and

```
d = [d1, d2, . . ., dr]
```

then the region defined by [d of R] has indices such that the ith coordinate ranges over the interval [l..u], where

$$[l..u] = \begin{cases} [u_i+1..u_i+d_i] & \text{if } d_i > 0 \\ [l_i..u_i] & \text{if } d_i = 0 \\ [l_i+d_i..l_i-1] & \text{if } d_i < 0 \end{cases} \qquad (*)$$

Thus, the sign of the direction determines whether the dimension is extended at the lower (negative) or the upper (positive) end of the base region's index range, and the magnitude indicates by how much; a zero value in a direction indicates that the whole interval for that dimension is inherited from the base region. Figure 3.1 shows examples.

Although the regions defined by the "of" operation are simply index sets, e.g., the regions of figure 3.1 define the following index sets,

```
[SW2  of R]  ≡ [ 9..10, -1..0]
[E2   of R]  ≡ [ 1.. 8, 9..10]
```

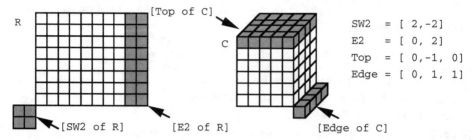

Figure 3.1
Examples of applying "of" to regions R=[1..8,1..8] and C=[1..4,1..5,1..5]

```
[Top  of  C]   ≡  [ 1.. 4,  0..0,  1..5]
[Edge of  C]   ≡  [ 1.. 4,  6..6,  6..6]
```

they differ in an important way from the equivalent regions declared directly. Specifically, because "of" regions specify the region relative to a base region, they can be used to give arrays *borders*. That is, when an array is declared over the base region and is then used in the context of an "of" region defined relative to that base region, the referenced elements are treated as part of the array. For example, using the definitions from figure 3.1, and assuming A and B are declared over the base region R,

```
[E2 of R]   A := 0.1;      -- initialize border columns to east
[E2 of R]   B := c*A;      -- Set B's border to A's scaled by c
```

reference the 9th and 10th columns of A and B. Though A and B were not originally declared to have these two columns, the use of the array names in the context of an "of" region augments the arrays with the region [E2 of R]. Thus, when a problem has "boundary conditions," the "of" region can establish bordering regions to hold the boundary values. It is not necessary (or advisable) to declare arrays "larger" to accommodate boundary values as is necessary in Fortran or C.

Summarizing, "of" defines a new region from a base region and a direction. The region is adjacent to and disjoint from the base in the given direction. If an "of" defines "new" indices for the variable on the left-hand side of the assignment on which it appears, storage is declared for those new border indices automatically, provided the region of the "of" expression is the same symbolic region name as was used to declare the array.

Using Directions with "@"

The "@" operator is used to implement the concept of "offset-referencing" or translation of arrays. Thus, in the Jacobi program, references to the nearest neighbors of A's elements were expressed as A@north, A@east, A@west and A@south.

In general, the "@" operator performs a uniform translation of a region's indices and then references those elements of the array. Thus, in the construction

```
[R]        . . . A@d . . .
```

the referenced elements of A (and possibly its borders) are those found by adding the direction d to each index tuple in R. The result of the expression is an array of the rank, size and index set of R. Thus, assuming R=[1..5,1..8], A is defined over R and has a one column eastern boundary defined, and the value in each *i,j* position is *j*, then

```
[R]        . . . A@E . . .
```

refers to the shaded items, given E = [0,1]

It must be emphasized that the rank, size and index set of the result of applying the "@" operator are determined by the region specifier, not the array. The array (and possibly its borders) simply supply the values to be referenced. Thus, certain uses of "@" will not result in an "array shift" or a spill to a border. To illustrate, consider the declarations,

```
region      R      = [1..3, 1..n];    --A 3 x n region
            Mid    = [2..2, 1..n];    --A 1 x n region

var         A3, B3: [R] integer;      --3 x n arrays

direction   above =  [-1, 0];         --Offset first index up
            below =  [ 1, 0];         --Offset first index down
```

which in the following statement

```
[Mid]   A3@above := B3@below;
```

assigns the third row of B3 to the first row of A3. The region Mid, which is a set of indices for the second row of the R region, is translated to indices for the first row by above and to indices for the last row by below. The elements transferred have the rank, size and index set of Mid.

In most programming languages, such a translation would be realized by iteratively referencing each element of the array using one or more nested loops, and for each tuple of indices, *(i,j, . . . , k),* a constant offset would be added when subscripting the array. ZPL's ability to operate on arrays in their entirety saves the tedious looping, and the use of symbolically named directions, e.g., `northeast`, avoids common errors in computing offsets in the subscripts, e.g., [i−1, j+1].

Whenever a region is applied to an array, it is necessary for all region indices to refer to declared and initialized array elements. For many uses of regions this is automatic, since the array declaration requires a region specifier, which is then used as the region specifier in the computations. When an "@" is used, however, it is typical for the references to spill beyond the base region of the array. As a heuristic, then, if the applicable region is the defiining region of the array, the operands using @ imply an earlier use of "of".

Comparison of "of" vs "@"

Notice that both "of" and "@" create regions from regions, but they perform this operation in different ways. Stated in words,

· "of" extends a region by defining an adjacent set of indices according to rule (*) above.

· "@" translates a region by adding the direction vector to each index of the base region.

The indices of an "of"-defined region are necessarily disjoint from the base region, while the indices of an "@" defined region (typically) overlap it. The distinction is easily illustrated by an example. Assume the declarations,

```
region      R   = [1..8, 1..8];
direction   N2  = [-2, 0];
            NE2 = [-2, 2];
            E2  = [ 0, 2];
var         A   : [R] integer;
```

then the relevant regions of A are illustrated in figure 3.2.

Borders

ZPL provides a convenient mechanism to implement two commonly occurring boundary conditions: mirrored and periodic. The operations are called `reflect` and `wrap`. Both require an "of"-defined region specifier as the border, in order that there be an unambiguous reference point.

The `wrap` operator has the general form

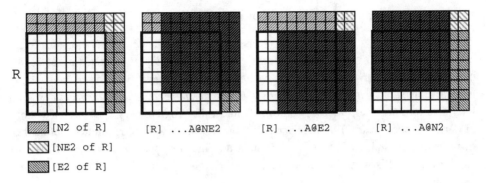

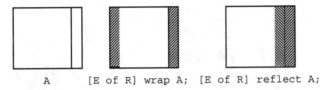

Figure 3.2
Comparison of regions specified using "of" and "@"

Figure 3.3
Examples of `wrap` and `reflect` for a 2D array A and direction E = [0,1]

[*d* of *R*]   wrap   *vars*;

where *vars* is a list of array identifiers, separated by commas. The effect of applying `wrap` to the d border of an array A is to set the border elements to be the values from the "opposite" side of the array, that is, as if they "wrap around." See figure 3.3. The general form of the `reflect` operation is

[*d* of *R*]   reflect *vars*;

where *vars* is a list of array identifiers, separated by commas. The effect of applying `reflect` to the d border of an array A is to set the elements of the boundary to be "mirrored around" the array's edge. See figure 3.3.

The operators are sufficiently intuitive that their rather complicated formal definitions will be omitted. Notice that in the figure, the "hatching" is meaningful. That is, in `wrap` the data is translated, preserving order, whereas in `reflect` the data is mirrored, reversing the order.

Array and Cartesian Coordinates for Directions

ZPL's interpretation of directions in terms of array coordinates rather than Cartesian coordinates leads to the simple, uniform rule for describing the semantics of region expressions: *A negative offset in a dimension refers to elements with lower index values in that dimension, while a positive offset refers to elements with higher indices.* This interpretation, however, troubles some first-time ZPL programmers, who prefer to think in Cartesian coordinates. But, this is not a problem because ZPL programmers define their own directions, and can therefore give them any meaning they wish *provided they are consistent.* (This is why ZPL does not come with built-in directions.) For example, the declarations

```
region FQ = [0..n, 0..n];      -- An n+1 x n+1 region
var Cart : [FQ] double;        -- A variable declaration

direction    plusx  = [ 1, 0]; -- Cartesian right
             plusy  = [ 0, 1]; -- Cartesian up
             minusx = [-1, 0]; -- Cartesian left
             minusy = [ 0,-1]; -- Cartesian down
```

used consistently, allow the `Cart` array to be thought of as though it were indexed like the first quadrant of the plane, i.e., the (0,0) element is conceptually in the lower left corner. So, for example,

```
[FQ]   ... Cart@plusy ...
```

can be thought of as the array of values translated one unit in the upward (positive y) direction of the plane, because when thinking of FQ as the lattice points in the first quadrant, [0,1] translates the points upwards. The fact that the ZPL compiler writers and possibly even the compiler itself interpret this differently is irrelevant. The association of the letter sequence "plusy" or "east" to [0,1] is completely arbitrary; it could be "moonward" or "bzz333". If the Cartesian interpretation is used consistently, no computational problems should arise.* Accordingly, programmers are encouraged to adopt whatever interpretation makes sense to them, and to include a comment to assist anyone who reads the program.

---

* Probably the only way a consistent use of alternate directions can be "exposed" is with the use of I/O, which is transmitted with the right-most-dimensions-varying-fastest rule applied to the least index of the region. Thus, in this example, the (0,0) element of Cart would be printed first. Users adopting an alternative set of directions may wish to preserve the illusion by restructuring their arrays before printing, postprocessing the output off-line or simply assuring that the visualization software accepts the ZPL output as given.

Promotion

Scalars can be used throughout ZPL as if they were arrays of the rank, size and index set of the region specifier for the operand with which they are composed. Scalars used in this role are said to be *promoted* to arrays. Thus, in the expression from the Jacobi program,

```
[R] Temp := (A@north+A@east+A@west+A@south)/4.0;
```

the scalar constant 4.0 is promoted to an array, implementing elementwise averaging, i.e., it becomes an array of 4.0's of the rank, size and shape of R. Scalar promotion applies to each occurrence, taking the form required by the situation in which it is used. Thus, if c is a scalar variable in

```
if dim = 1
  then [V] V1 := c*V2;
  else [W] W1 := c*W2;
end;
```

the promotion is to an array of rank, size and index set of V in the then-clause and to W in the else-clause. Scalar promotion does not apply to a scalar on the left-hand side of an assignment statement. Thus

```
[R] c := A; -- ILLEGAL, scalar promotion not allowed on lhs
```

is not legal. (See the reduce operator below.)

Promotion also applies to sequential functions. Examples of sequential functions are the built-in numerical functions such as sin(), or user defined functions not employing array concepts in their definitions, e.g., concepts defined in this chapter. For example, in the statement

```
err := max<< abs(A - Temp);
```

from the Jacobi program, the (floating point) absolute value function, abs, is promoted to accept an array, the result of A-Temp, as its actual parameter. As with variable promotion, function promotion applies to each occurrence, as the situation requires. The meaning is to apply the scalar function to the operand(s) for each index value of the region, i.e., elementwise.

Index1, Index2, . . .

In ZPL (parallel) arrays cannot be explicitly indexed. This provides a significant amount of "under constrained" computation for which a compiler can plan efficient execution.

This is one of the properties of ZPL that allows it to execute fast on parallel computers. However, it is often useful to use the index value in a computation. For this reason there are compiler-provided constant arrays, known as Index*d*, that contain in each indexed position a value of that index. (There are also "indexed arrays," discussed in chapter 5.)

For example, assuming V is a one dimensional region, V = [1..n], and V1 is a one dimensional variable defined over V, then the occurrence of Index1 in the statement

```
[V]    . . . V1 + Index1 . . .
```

is an n element vector containing in the ith position the value i, i.e.,

```
Index1 ≡ 1    2    3    . . . n
```

The Index*d* arrays are constant, they cannot be modified. Thus, constructions like

```
Index1 := . . .;        -- ILLEGAL, cannot modify Indexd
```

are prohibited.

In general, the Index*d* constant arrays are used by replacing *d* with a numerical value, say 2, specifying a dimension. The options are, therefore,

Index1   dimension 1 indices

Index2   dimension 2 indices

Index3   dimension 3 indices

. . .

Indexd   dimension d indices

. . .

Indexr   dimension r indices

where r is the highest dimension of any declared region of the program. Clearly, the r limit can be different for different programs.

The value of Index*d* is an array of the indices of the *d* dimension as determined by context. Thus, the shape and size of the array are the shape and size of the operand region applicable to the operand with which it is being combined. For example, if R = [1..3, 1..4] is a rank 2 region and Any is a two dimensional array over these indices, then

```
[R]       ... Any + Index1 ...
```

adds the row index to each element of Any, i.e., in this instance Index1 has the value

```
1   1   1   1
2   2   2   2
3   3   3   3
```

Contrast this with the occurrence of Index1 applied to a rank 1 array above. In each case, the shape and size of the Index*d* constant array are given by the shape and size of R, the applicable region for the variable with which it is composed.

Continuing the example,

```
[R]       ... Any + Index2 ...
```

adds the column index to each element of Any, i.e., in this instance Index2 has the value

```
1   2   3   4
1   2   3   4
1   2   3   4
```

So, Index*d* extracts the dth items from the index tuple.

In general, if Index*d* is combined with an operand of rank r, the applicable region specifier that determines Index*d*'s size and shape is the rank r region specifier. (It is an error if $d > r$.) As a further example, if V = [1..n] is a region, and V1 and V2 are rank 1 arrays, and W = [-5..5, 1..5] is a region and W1 and W2 are rank 2 arrays, then the statement

```
[V][W] if dim = 1
            then V1 := Index1*V2;   -- Ref 1D indices
            else W1 := Index1*W2;   -- Ref first dim indices
         end;
```

causes (among other things) the first element of V2 to be multiplied by 1 if dim = 1, or the first element of W2 to be multiplied by -5 otherwise.

For a square region R = [1..n, 1..n], the statement

```
[R]       Identity := Index1=Index2;
```

results in the identity matrix,

```
1   0   0   0
0   1   0   0
0   0   1   0
0   0   0   1
```

when n = 4, since the comparison of the Index*d* values is true (1) only on the diagonal.

The `Index`*d* constant arrays can be used in assignment statements,

```
[R]  X := Index2;        -- Set X to second dim indices
```

where the applicable region specifier is given by the left-hand side variable. Since the shape and size of an `Index`*d* constant array are determined by the operand with which it is composed, there are a few cases where the applicable region specifier cannot be inferred, e.g.,

```
s := +<<Index1;        -- Undefined use of Index1
```

and so the value is undefined.

Finally, it is frequently useful to initialize a multi-dimensional array such that in the ith position enumerated, say, in row-major order there is the value i. Row-major-order enumerates the items so the right-most indices change fastest, e.g., like an odometer. This can be computed easily and efficiently using the `Index`*d* arrays. Assuming R is a region with 1-origin indexing, i.e., the indices in each dimension begin with 1, the statement

```
[R]  Irmo := (Index1-1)*dim2size+Index2;
                            -- Init. to row-major indices
```

produces the array

```
1    2    3    4
5    6    7    8
9   10   11   12
```

if `dim2size` ≡ 4. If R is not 1-origin, then the obvious corrections are required.

`Index`*d* arrays are only logicial. The compiler does not allocate memory or explicitly create the `Index`*d* arrays, so they are very efficient to use.

Reduce and Scan

ZPL has two functional forms that can be used in global computations: reduce and scan. Both forms apply a function accumulatively to an array argument. Thus, `+<<A` finds the sum of the elements in A, i.e., *reduces* A to its sum. The forms are as follows:

Reduce	Name	Scan
+<<	plus	+||
*<<	times	*||
max<<	maximum	max||

min<<	minimum	min||
&<<	and	&||
|<<	or	|||

In general, for an array A the result of op\|\|A is an array of the shape and size of the applicable region in which the ith element is the op-accumulation of the first i elements of the array, where the ordering is given by row-major order. Thus, if for the applicable region of A

```
A ≡ 1   2   3
    1   2   3
```

then the plus-scan of A

```
+||A ≡ 1   3   6
       7   9  12
```

and

```
max||A ≡ 1   2   3          min||A ≡ 1   1   1
         3   3   3                   1   1   1
```

In general, for an array A, the result of the reduction op<<A is a scalar that is the op-accumulation of the whole array, i.e., the last element of op\|\|A. Thus, +<<A ≡ 12, max<<A ≡ 3, and min<<A ≡ 1, given the previous definition of A.

The operations available for use with scan and reduce are associative and commutative as mathematical operations. They are treated as such in ZPL, i.e., the compiler reserves the right to accumulate the elements in any order that realizes the definition. However, in the finite precision of floating point arithmetic, associativity is not strictly true for plus and times under all circumstances.

The default is to apply reduce and scan to the entire applicable region of the operand. In addition, a partial reduce or partial scan can be specified to operate on a subset of the dimensions.

Partial scan is expressed by placing dimension specifiers—dimension numbers in square brackets—to the right of the function symbol, before the operand. The specifier indicates which dimension(s) are to be scanned. Thus,

```
ColSum := +||[1] A;   -- Add columns
```

is a plus-scan along the first dimension, i.e., the columns are added, assuming A is 2D. As expected, a partial scan will produce a result that is the same shape and size as the operand. Partial reduce is slightly more complicated, since the number of dimensions in the result is logically smaller than the operand, and so it is treated in chapter 5.

If more than one dimension are to be partially scanned, the items in brackets are separated by commas, e.g., +||[1,2] A. The dimensions are scanned in the (left-to-right) order given in brackets. Since "wrapping" is part of scanning, the order that the dimensions are scanned matters. See figure 3.4. Thus, for 2D arrays, op|| [2,1] gives a row-major order complete op-scan, i.e., is equivalent to op||, and op|| [1,2] gives a column-major order complete op-scan. These are different from the consecutive application of one dimensional scans, since separate scans will not wrap. Notice that as mathematical operations the different orders of application of consecutive separate scans are all equivalent. This is not strictly true in the finite precision of a computer's floating point arithmetic.

To summarize, figure 3.4 gives the logical order of accumulation for partial scan operations.

```
1   1   1   1        1   2   3   4        1   1   1   1        1    2    3    4
1   1   1   1        1   2   3   4        2   2   2   2        5    6    7    8
1   1   1   1        1   2   3   4        3   3   3   3        9   10   11   12
       A                +||[2]A              +|| [1]A                +||A


1   2   3    4       1   4   7   10       1   2   3    4       1   2   3    4
5   6   7    8       2   5   8   11       2   4   6    8       2   4   6    8
9  10  11   12       3   6   9   12       3   6   9   12       3   6   9   12
   +||[2,1]A            +||[1,2]A         +||[1](+||[2])   ≡  +||[2](+||[1]A)
```

Figure 3.4
Logical order of accumulation for scan

4 Program Structure and Examples

The goal of this chapter is to illustrate the constructs presented in the last chapter, and to introduce ZPL programming idioms and style. In order to enable readers to run sample programs, basics of program structure and I/O are treated first.

ZPL Programs

Though there is considerable flexibility in how ZPL programs are organized, the programmer must observe a few rules regarding program structure.

Figure 4.1 shows the general schema of a ZPL program.

In the schema the non-italic text must be given literally, including the punctuation. The italicized text is to be replaced with syntactically correct code meeting the italicized description. Items in braces are optional. *Pname* is an identifier that is the name of the program, and must match in its two occurrences. The Preamble items can appear in any order. Notice how the Jacobi computation of figure 1.2 fits into this structure.

The `config var` declaration section is used to specify parameters to the computation such as array sizes, convergence tolerances, etc. The `config var` parameters are assigned default values in the declaration that can be changed on the command line when

```
program Pname;

{config var declarations;}          --
{constant declarations;}            --
{type declarations;}                --
{direction declarations;}           -- Preamble
{region declarations;}              --
{var declarations;}                 --
{Procedure_definitions;}            --


procedure Pname();                  -- Entry point procedure
Main_program_definition;
```

Figure 4.1
Structure of ZPL programs

the program is invoked. This allows the program to vary from run to run without recompilation. The declaration has the form

```
config var
    ident1     : type1 = val1;
       . . .
    identn     : typen = valn;
```

where the italicized material must be replaced as follows: *identi* is an identifier, *typei* is its value type (see chapter 2), and *vali* is its default value, to be used unless changed at execution time. The `config var` parameters can be used throughout the program, including in the remaining declarations, but they cannot be changed, i.e. they cannot appear on the left-hand side of an assignment, nor be passed as `var` parameters to a procedure, see chapter 5.

To change the value of a `config var` on the command line for UNIX systems, use the syntax

```
-sname=val
```

for each configuration variable *name* that is to be assigned a new *val*. Thus, for the Jacobi Iteration in figure 1.2, which has the configuration variables n and `delta`, the invocation

```
jacobi -sn=25 -sdelta=.0001
```

resets both variables to new values. Further details on changing the default values of `config var` parameters are available as part of the compiler installation documentation.

Following the configuration variables are other global declarations, including `constant` declarations, `region` declarations (chapter 3), `type` declarations (chapter 5), `direction` declarations (chapter 3), and `var` declarations. The `constant` declarations have the same form as the `config var` declarations above, e.g.

```
constant sisters : integer = 7;
```

and the `var` declarations simply list the variables of each type.

Though these declarations can be dense lists, it is recommended programming style to consider how formatting might make the variable enumeration clearer. For example,

```
var       x_x_,x0x_,x_x0,x0x0,x_y_,x0y_,x_y0,x0y0:sbyte;
```

is identical to

```
var      x_x_, x_y_,        -- not present
         x0x_, x0y_,        -- single left
         x_x0, x_y0,        -- single right
         x0x0, x0y0:        -- filled
                     sbyte; -- range is -128 to 127
```

except for comments and white space, but the formatting improves the readability, makes it easier to verify that there are no notational errors, and provides information to the program reader.

The procedures of the program are declared at this point. One of the procedures, usually the last or the first to be declared, is the procedure whose name is the same as the program. This is the main program or "entry point" procedure, i.e. the place where the computation begins.

The `config var`, `constant`, `type`, `region`, and `direction` declarations are global to the program, and are therefore declared before the procedure declarations. Variables can be declared either in the preamble or in the procedures, including the main procedure. Most scientific and engineering computations will have global variables representing the problem state. These are usually referenced by most or many of the program's procedures, and their space needs may dominate the memory requirements of the program. It is common to declare these variables in the preamble as part of the context of the computation, and to declare all other variables within the procedures.

All ZPL source code must appear in a single file, though files can be included. That is, a line of the form

```
#include "filename"
```

will be replaced by the text in the file *filename* in the ZPL source file at the site of the statement. Separate compilation is not presently supported.

Basic I/O

Programs must print out results, and most must also read in data. ZPL provides input/output facilities, the most basic forms of which are treated here.

Text I/O   Because ZPL was developed in a UNIX environment, three files are always open, `zin`, `zout` and `zerr`, coresponding to UNIX's `stdin`, `stdout` and `stderr`. Programs can use other files for input and output by declaring a variable of type `file`,

```
var f : file;      -- Declare variable for file descriptor
```

which is used to hold a file's descriptor. The file descriptor is set using the open() procedure,

```
f := open("exprdata", "r");    -- Open a file for reading
```

where the first parameter is the name of the file in quotation marks, and the second parameter is one of three alternatives, "r", "w", "a", stating that data is to be read, written or appended to the file. The open() procedure returns a descriptor for the file that is to be used for all subsequent references to the file, or 0 if the opening operation was unsuccessful, e.g., the file could not be found. Notice that open() is not a parallel procedure, so it requires no region.

Data are read from or written to files using the procedures,

```
read({file,} vars);
write({file,} vars);
writeln({file,} vars);
```

where *file* is the optional file descriptor, and *vars* is a list of identifier names participating in the I/O, separated by commas. If the file descriptor is not specified, zin is used for reading and zout is used for writing. The write() and writeln() procedures differ only in that the latter writes a newline character after all of the variables are written.

The *vars* list can contain either sequential or parallel variable names. If (parallel) arrays are given, then appropriate region specifiers must apply to the statements. The entire applicable region of the array is read or written, with the items assigned positions in row-major order, or more generally in rightmost-index-changes-fastest order. For example,

```
    read(n);                      -- Get problem size from zin
[R] read(f, A);                   -- Fill region R of A from file f
[R] write(fdata, Alast);          -- Save results in output file
[V] writeln("Control Vector: ", C);   -- Echo inputs to zout
    writeln("MegaFLOPS :", f10to6);    -- Report performance
```

are sample input/output statements.

Files other than zin and zout should be closed after their last use. The command is close(*file*), where *file* is the file descriptor returned from the open() command. So,

```
close(f);     -- Finish up with file f
```

completes the use of the file f. Notice, close() is not a parallel procedure. Check the compiler installation documentation for further information on I/O.

Binary I/O ZPL also supports binary I/O. Though binary files are not conveniently readable by humans and are not portable to different machines, binary I/O has the advantage of being faster than textual I/O and more precise because it is a direct copy of the computer's internal representation. Accordingly, it is ideal for check-pointing files and for out-of-core applications.

Binary I/O simply extends the concepts used for textual I/O. The procedures `open()` and `close()` are unchanged. The binary versions of the I/O routines are

```
bread({file,} vars);
bwrite({file,} vars);
```

where *file* is the (optional) file descriptor returned by `open()`, and *vars* is a list of the variables or expressions to be read or written. As with text I/O the applicable region specifier determines what portion of each array in the variable list is to be read or written. ZPL's binary I/O commands generally conform to the `fread` of `fwrite` of the underlying C platform. Also, on many platforms text and binary I/O can be intermixed in one file.

As an example, check-pointing is accomplished by a instruction sequence of the form

```
    ckpt := open("dump", "w");
    bwrite(ckpt, iter,       -- save iteration number
                 corrct,     -- save accumulated correction
                 lastx       -- save x position of last step
                 lasty);     -- save y position of last step
[R]bwrite(ckpt, A, B, C,     -- save entire
                 D, E, F);   --    state arrays
    close(ckpt);             -- wrap up
```

Repeated execution of this code will overwrite the last instance of the file. An alternating file name scheme—`dump1` and `dump2`—can be used to protect against the unlikely possibility that the machine crashes during the ckeck pointing.

Example Computations

In this section ZPL will be used to solve "typical" scientific and engineering calculations. The emphasis is on illustrating standard ZPL idioms, i.e. showing characteristic constructs and styles for solving problems:

· Computing over entire arrays without any indexing.

· Substituting computations over logical vectors for `if` statements.

· Comparing alternative solutions based on expected performance.

Though these techniques are highlighted here, they are all intuitive, and easily understood and used.

Sample Statistics

The computation to be illustrated is that of finding the mean and standard deviation of a set of data values. The overall structure of the program is to read the data, compute the statistics, and print the results. The program is shown in figure 4.2.

The programmer has defined items, the size of the problem, to have the default value 100, and this value is used to declare the region R. No direction declarations are needed for this calculation. In the header of the main procedure Sample is declared together with two scalars, mu and sigma. The statistics are computed by a direct application of their defining formulae.

The mean, μ, defined as

$$\mu = \Sigma_i \, Sample_i \, / n$$

is computed by

```
mu := +<<(Sample/n);        -- Mean
```

where the summation is accomplished by the plus-reduction operation over the Sample array. Notice that because of the precedence of the operators (table 2.1), the plus-reduction binds more tightly than the division, so parentheses are required if each Sample item is to be divided by n. Eliminating the parentheses performs a single division after summing Sample, which may be somewhat more precise at the risk of a greater possibility of

```
1 program Sample_Stats;
2 /* Program computing the mean and standard deviation of a sample */
3
4 config var n : integer = 100;             -- Problem size
5 region   R = [1..n];                      -- Problem space
6
7 procedure Sample_Stats();                 -- Start of Program
8 var      Sample : [R] float;              -- Declare data array
9          mu, sigma : float;               -- Declare scalars
10
11 [R]begin
12     read(Sample);                        -- Input from zin
13     mu    := +<<(Sample/n);              -- Mean
14     sigma := sqrt(+<<((Sample-mu)^2/n)); -- Std deviation
15     writeln("Mean: ", mu);               -- Print
16     writeln("Standard Deviation: ", sigma);  --   results
17 end;
```

Figure 4.2
Sample statistics program

```
 1 program Coefficient;
 2 /* Compute the means and correlation coefficient of two samples */
 3
 4 config var n : integer = 100;               -- Problem size
 5 region        V = [1..n];                    -- Problem space
 6
 7 procedure Coefficient();                     -- Start of Program
 8     var Sample1, Sample2 : [V] float;        -- Declare data array
 9           mu1, mu2, r : float;               -- Declare scalars
10              f1, f2 : file;                  -- File name variables
11
12 [V]begin
13     f1 := open("Expr1","r"); read(f1,Sample1); --Data from file Expr1
14     f2 := open("Expr2","r"); read(f2,Sample2); --Data from file Expr2
15     mu1 := +<<(Sample1/n);                   -- First sample mean
16     mu2 := +<<(Sample2/n);                   -- Second sample mean
17     Sample1 := Sample1 - mu1;                -- Center about mean
18     Sample2 := Sample2 - mu2;                -- Same for next sample
19     r := (+<<(Sample1*Sample2))              -- Correlation coeff'nt
20         / sqrt((+<<(Sample1^2))*(+<<(Sample2^2)));
21     writeln("Sample means: ", mu1, mu2);     -- Print
22     writeln("Correlation coefficient: ", r); --    results
23     close(f1); close(f2);                    -- Wrap up for exit
24     end;
```

Figure 4.3
Computing the correlation coefficient

overflow. Parentheses showing the groupings are recommended as good programming practice.

The standard deviation, σ, defined as

$$\sigma = \sqrt{\Sigma_i \, (Sample_i - \mu)^2} \, / \, n$$

is translated directly into

```
sigma := sqrt(+<<((Sample-mu)^2/n));        -- Std deviation
```

where the sqrt function computes the square root. Notice that subtracting mu from Sample has the effect of promoting the scalar to an array with shape and size given by [R], and then subtracting corresponding elements. The results are printed and the program exits.

Correlation Coefficient

Figure 4.3 illustrates a program that is quite similar to Sample_Stats. Coefficient finds the means of two samples and computes their correlation coefficient,

$$r = \frac{\Sigma_i \, (Sample1_i - \mu_1)(Sample2_i - \mu_2)}{\sqrt{\Sigma_i \, (Sample1_i - \mu_1)^2 \cdot \Sigma_i \, (Sample2_i - \mu_2)^2}}$$

on lines 19–20.

One difference with `Sample_Stat` is that `Coefficient` reads in its data from files. The files, which are expected to be called "Expr1" and "Expr2," are specified by a call to the procedure `open()` that returns a file descriptor. This is assigned to a variable of type `file`, and used in the subsequent `read()` and `close()` procedures. Though the program works if the files are not closed before exit, it is a good policy to do so. As before, the results are written to `zout`, since no file is specified in the `writeln()` statements.

The program is very similar to `Sample_Stats`. All computation in the body is performed within the scope of the region specifier `[V]`, so all array operations apply to all n items of the two arrays. In lines 15–16 the plus-reduction operation is used to sum the elements to compute the two means. Then, in lines 17–18 these means are promoted to n element arrays to match the `Sample` arrays, and corresponding elements are subtracted. An alternative way to express these two computations employs ZPL's extended assignment operators,

```
Sample1 -= mu1;      -- Center about mean
Sample2 -= mu2;      -- Same for next sample
```

The correlation coefficient is computed in an expression that breaks across lines 19–20. Notice that the second line starts with the divide operator. It is helpful to begin continuation lines with an operator as a visual cue to indicate a multiline statement, but of course, it is not required. Finally, the results are printed out.

Histogram

Computing the values for a histogram of a data set is straightforward. First the interval spanned by the entire data set of `Values` is found by determining the smallest and largest elements,

```
small := min<<Values;
big   := max<<Values;
```

using the reduction operators. If this range is to be divided into b equal size bins, then each bin has a `size` determined by

```
size := (big - small)/b;
```

To assign the `Values` to one of the b equal sized bins, it is expedient to shift the values by subtracting `small` so the smallest is zero, then to divide the `size` into each item,

```
BinNo := ceil((Values-small)/size);
```

rounding-up the fractional part to the next highest integer. This results in $BinNo_i$ containing the bin number for $Values_i$.

This assigns each of the `Values` to the proper bin except those items equal to `small`, the low end point of the whole interval. They are assigned to the nonexistent bin 0. Assuming such elements are to be assigned to bin 1, it is necessary to increment all `BinNos` having a value 0. It is possible to fix up these entries with an `if`-statement that tests for 0 and then increments it. But, it is also possible to write

```
BinNo := BinNo + !BinNo;     -- Put "small" elements in bin 1
```

which uses the fact that nonzero `BinNo` values are treated as logical true and 0 `BinNo` values are treated as logical false. Thus, the negation `!BinNo` yields a vector of trues (1) and falses (0) where 0s and nonzeroes occur in `BinNo`. By adding these to `BinNo`, the 0s are incremented.

For example, if

$$b \equiv 3 \text{ and } Values \equiv 6.3 \ -4.2 \ 0.0 \ 1.9 \ 5.4 \ -2.2 \ -4.2 \ -2.2$$

then

```
small := min<<Values;       -- small  ≡ -4.2
big   := max<<Values;       -- big    ≡  6.3
size  := (big-small)/b;     -- size   ≡  3.5
BinNo := ceil((Values-small)/size);
                            -- BinNo ≡ 3  0  2  2  3  1  0  1
BinNo := BinNo + !BinNo;    -- !BinNo ≡ 0  1  0  0  0  0  1  0
```

producing a final value

```
BinNo ≡ 3  1  2  2  3  1  1  1
```

as intended.

This programming technique—using the addition of a Boolean vector as a substitute for an `if`-statement—is an example of computing with logical vectors. This is a recommended approach not only because of the clean and succinct program, it uses computation instead of control to achieve the result. Since modern pipelined computers are slowed by the "control jumps" typical of `if`-statements, using logical vectors will likely result in faster code.

```
 1 program Histo;
 2 /*
 3     The n values read from zin are grouped into b equal
 4     sized intervals over their range, counted and printed out.
 5     Values on the boundaries are associated with the higher interval.
 6                                                                           */
 7 config var n : integer = 100;      -- Size of data
 8             b : integer = 8;        -- Number of intervals in histogram
 9 region      S = [1..n];             -- The index space of the data
10
11 procedure Histo();                  -- Entry point
12 var       small,                    -- Smallest value
13              big,                    -- Largest value
14            size : float;            -- Interval size of bin
15     count, i : integer;             -- Integer scalars
16     Values   : [S] float;           -- Data value array
17     BinNo    : [S] ushortint;       -- Bin numbers are nonnegative
18
19 [S]begin
20     read(Values);                   -- Get the data from zin
21     small := min<<Values;           -- Get smallest value
22     big   := max<<Values;           -- Get largest value
23     size  := (big-small)/b;         -- Figure size of the intervals
24     BinNo := ceil((Values-small)/size);
25                                     -- Compute position, round up
26     BinNo :=  BinNo + !BinNo;       --Include lo endpoints in first bin
27     writeln("Histogram of ", n,
28                 " values, ranging from ", small,
29                 " to ", big,
30                 " grouped into ", b,
31                 " intervals of size ", size);
32     for i := 1 to b do
33       count := +<<(BinNo = i);      -- Count how many in this interval
34       writeln("Interval ",small + (i-1)*size,
35                 " : ", small + i*size,
36                 " = ", count);
37     end;
38   end;
```

Figure 4.4
Program to print the count of samples in b equal-sized bins

In the Histo program shown in figure 4.4 there is a second application of computing with logical vectors. After writing out the header information for the computation (lines 27–31), a for-loop is entered in which on the ith iteration, the number of elements in bin i are counted and then printed. To count the number of elements in bin i, BinNo is compared to i producing a logical vector over which a sum reduction is applied yielding the number of elements in the bin

```
count := +<<(BinNo = i);
```

Again, this is an efficient alternative to the use of an if-statement A variant of this histogram program is given in chapter 6.

Uniform Convolution

In this application the values stored in the 512×512 array are picture elements or *pixels*. The uniform convolution problem is to treat every point in the image as the lower right corner of a $x \times y$ box of pixels, and to store the weighted sum of the elements of the box into that position. Perhaps the most straightforward solution is to shift the array around, adding up the pixels. But there is an ingenious solution using the scan, which will also be considered.

Shift-and-Add Solution

This solution of the uniform convolution computation conceptually shifts the image to the right, accumulating in each position the pixel values of the row to its left. These values, i.e. the box's row sums, are then shifted down and accumulated, scaled and written out. The program is shown in figure 4.5.

The program begins by defining the default sizes of the box base, boxb, box height, boxh, and weight, w, since these quantities will tend to be the same from run to run. By being declared as config vars, however, their values can be changed on the command line when the program is executed. Im is declared to be an unsigned byte array, allowing the pixels to have at most 256 distinct values, and BoxSum, the array that will accumulate the values from the various positions, is declared ushortint. This specification allows for boxes with area up to 256 pixels without overflow, because if $\text{boxh} \times \text{boxb} = box$ $area \le 256$ then the

$$largest\ pixel\ value \times box\ area \le 255 \times 256 = (2^8-1) \times 2^8 < 2^{16}-1$$

the typical precision of unsigned short integers. Notice that because BoxSum is an integer value, the scaling (line 34) will truncate any fractional parts.

The program begins by opening a file that has the default name "Image", which can be changed on the command line, and reading the contents into Im.

The computation begins by initializing to 0 the west and north boundaries of T, the copy of the image (and later the row sums) that will be shifted around to accomplish the summation. The shifting will first go to the right, and then downwards, which means that 0's will be introduced into T from the west and north boundaries.

BoxSum is initialized to Im, which would be the final result for a degenerate 1×1 box, and T is initialized to the image. Shifting to the right is implemented in the for-loop (lines 25–28), yielding the effect of summing across the rows of a box of width boxb. This intermediate result is then assigned to T, and the columns are added up. Since the column above a given position contains the sums of the rows of the box, this produces the result, which is then scaled and written out.

```
 1 program UniConv_Shift;
 2 config var   N : integer = 512;          -- No. pixels in 1 dim.
 3             boxb : ushortint = 4;         -- Default size box base
 4             boxh : ushortint = 4;         -- Default size box height
 5                w : ushortint = 16;        -- Default weight
 6         filename : string = "Image";      -- Name of input file
 7 region       I = [1..N, 1..N];            -- Problem space
 8 var         Im : [I] ubyte;               -- Image of pixels
 9      BoxSum, T : [I] ushortint;           -- Result and temp
10           fptr : file;                    -- Unix file descriptor
11
12 direction west = [ 0,-1];
13           north = [-1, 0];
14
15 procedure UniConv_Shift();                 -- Entry point
16 var           i : integer;                -- Loop variable
17
18          [I] begin                        -- Refer to entire image
19                fptr := open(filename,"r"); -- Locate the file
20                read(fptr,Im);             -- Get the image
21   [west of I]  T := 0;                     -- Init west boundary
22   [north of I] T := 0;                     -- Init north boundary
23                BoxSum := Im;              -- Init BoxSum w/1st val
24                T := Im;                    -- T will shift around
25                for i := 1 to boxb - 1 do -- Across box ...
26                  T := T@west;             -- Shift image L-to-R
27                  BoxSum := BoxSum + T;    -- Accumulate
28                end;                        -- ... sweep rows
29                T := BoxSum;                -- Init T w/ box row sums
30                for i := 1 to boxh - 1 do  -- Across box ...
31                  T := T@north;            -- Shift row sums down
32                  BoxSum := BoxSum + T;    -- Accumulate
33                end;                        -- ... sweep columns
34                BoxSum := BoxSum/w;         -- Weight entries
35                writeln(BoxSum);            -- Print results to zout
36                close(fptr);                -- Close up
37              end;
```

Figure 4.5
Shift and Add solution to uniform convolution

Scan Solution

If the box size can be fixed at compile time, the programmer has available an alternative implementation based on the scan operation. Rather than adding up the rows and columns of the box, the basic idea is to use the scan to sum across the rows and columns of the whole image, and to derive the BoxSum by performing some simple arithmetic on these values. Figure 4.6 shows a uniform convolution solution using scan for a fixed 4×4 box.

The first difference is that BoxSum must be declared to be an unsigned integer, because summing over the entire array means that the magnitudes of the intermediate terms can be larger than can be represented in a shortint. A second difference is that the declarations for the directions (lines 10–12) are larger. These correspond to the size of

```
 1 program UniConv_Scan;                        -- No. pixels in 1 dim.
 2 config var   N : integer = 512;             -- Weight
 3              w : integer = 16;               -- Problem space
 4 region       I = [1..N, 1..N];              -- Image array
 5 var         Im : [I] ubyte;                 -- Result array
 6         BoxSum : [I] uinteger;              -- Name of input file
 7       filename : string;                    -- Unix file descriptor
 8           fptr : file;
 9
10 direction west = [ 0,-4];                    --\
11            north = [-4, 0];                  -- Box specifications
12            NW    = [-4,-4];                  --/
13
14 procedure UniConv_Scan();                    -- Entry point
15 [I]              begin                       -- Refer to the entire image
16 [west  of I]    BoxSum := 0;                -- Initialize the
17 [NW    of I]    BoxSum := 0;                --   boundaries of the
18 [north of I]    BoxSum := 0;                --     result to 0
19                 write("Image? ");read(filename);--Get name from zin
20                 fptr := open(filename,"r");-- Locate the file
21                 read(fptr,Im);              -- Get the image
22                 BoxSum := +||[2] Im;        -- Find row sums
23                 BoxSum := +||[1] BoxSum;-- Find column sums
24                 BoxSum := BoxSum - BoxSum@north -- Correct row sums
25                       - BoxSum@west    -- Correct column sums
26                       + BoxSum@NW;      -- NW subt'd twice, add in
27                 BoxSum := BoxSum/w;         -- Weight entries
28                 writeln(BoxSum);            -- Print results to zout
29                 close(fptr);                -- Button up
30               end;
```

Figure 4.6
Scan solution for the uniform convolution

the box rather than the unit of motion as they did in the shift-and-add solution. When the border initialization is specified (lines 16–18), these directions produce somewhat "thicker" borders

```
0 0 0 0 0 0 0 0 0
0 0 0 0 0 0 0 0 0
0 0 0 0 0 0 0 0 0
0 0 0 0 0 0 0 0 0
0 0 0 0┌───────────┐
0 0 0 0│           │
0 0 0 0│           │
0 0 0 0│  BoxSum   │
0 0 0 0│           │
0 0 0 0│           │
0 0 0 0└───────────┘
```

than the 1-wide borders of the shift-and-add solution.

After reading in the image, the program proceeds to compute the row and column sums using partial scans, i.e. scans that apply over one dimension only (chapter 3). Recall that the dimension over which the sum is performed is given in brackets (lines 22–23), so $+||[2]$ adds across rows, while, $+||[1]$ adds down columns.

The logic of the computation is simple. By plus-scanning the rows of Im (line 22), and then plus-scanning the columns of that result (line 23), each position contains the sum of itself and all pixels to the north and west. The values for these elements are the sum of the entire array to their northwest. For all elements with indices larger than four in either dimension, this is too much. So, the value from four rows above is subtracted (line 24), as is the value four columns to the left (line 25). However, this has subtracted the values to the northwest twice, so they must be added back in again (line 26), as the following example, using an array of 1 pixels, illustrates

```
1  1  1  1  1  1           1  2  3  4  5  6
1  1  1  1  1  1           1  2  3  4  5  6
1  1  1  1  1  1           1  2  3  4  5  6
1  1  1  1  1  1           1  2  3  4  5  6
1  1  1  1  1  1           1  2  3  4  5  6
        Im                     Line 22
```

```
1  2  3  4  5  6           1  2  3  4  5  6
2  4  6  8 10 12           2  4  6  8 10 12
3  6  9 12 15 18           3  6  9 12 15 18
4  8 12 16 20 24           4  8 12 16 20 24
5 10 15 20 25 30           4  8 12 16 20 24
      Line 23                   Line 24
```

```
1  2  3  4  4  4           1  2  3  4  5  5
2  4  6  8  8  8           2  4  6  8  8  8
3  6  9 12 12 12           3  6  9 12 12 12
4  8 12 16 16 16           4  8 12 16 16 16
4  8 12 16 15 14           4  8 12 16 16 16
      Line 25                   Line 26
```

Restoring the northwest component is required because the original value of BoxSum, as of line 23, is used throughout the computation of lines 24–26. As an exercise, the reader can verify that had the rows above and the columns to the left been subtracted off in separate statements, say with

```
BoxSum := BoxSum - BoxSum@north;
BoxSum := BoxSum - BoxSum@west;
```

no "northwest" correction would have been required. This is because the separate statements update the Boxsum value.

If the box size is known at compile time, the programmer has a choice of implementations. Which is preferable depends on the box size. For small boxes, e.g., 2 × 2, the shift solution is better since it reduces data motion. As the box size grows, however, the pair of scans becomes more efficient.

Counting Connected Components

The problem considered is counting the "connected components" of an image that is represented as a two dimensional array of binary pixels. Two 1's are in the same connected component if there is a path between them composed only of 1's, where the "steps" permitted in the path are any of the eight compass directions. This is the 8-way connected components definition; there is also a 4-way definition as well.

The program to count 8-way connected components will illustrate how ZPL programming benefits from thinking globally. The solution [Cypher *et al.* 90] relies on the "amazing" shrinking operator due to Levialdi. This morphological transformation preserves connectedness while reducing the size of a component. It is applied iteratively. The pixels are simultaneously rewritten to form the next iteration according to the following rule:

Levialdi Shrinking Operator (8-way): Pixels simultaneously change from one iteration to the next according to the rule:

$$1 \begin{cases} \text{remains 1 if there is a 1 to its west, northwest or north, } (1{\to}1) & \text{(a)} \\ \text{becomes 0 if there are 0's to its west, northwest and north } (1{\to}0) & \text{(b)} \end{cases}$$

$$0 \begin{cases} \text{becomes 1 if there are 1's to its west and north } (0{\to}1) & \text{(c)} \\ \text{remains 0 if there is a 0 to its west or north } (0{\to}0) & \text{(d)} \end{cases}$$

As the array is iteratively rewritten the connected components "shrink" to the lower right-hand corner of their bounding boxes, at which point they "disappear" on the next step. Figure 4.7 shows an example.

The strategy used in the algorithm is to apply the Levialdi operator iteratively until the array has no more 1's. Whenever connected components "disappear" they are counted. The only subtlety is to recognize the difference between 1's that are changed to 0's in the course of normal shrinking, i.e. due to rule (b), and the 1's that are changed to 0's in connection with a disappearance. The difference can be recognized by testing for the following conditions:

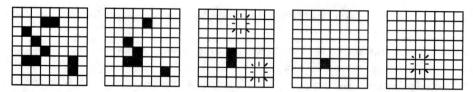

Figure 4.7
Example of shrinking connected components. The three components "disappear" where the "bursts" are shown

Disappearance: A disappearance occurs at a position that is 0 on the present iteration, if it was 1 on the previous iteration, and on the previous iteration there were no 1's in adjacent positions to its east, southeast, or south.

The condition excludes 1→0 transitions where a 1 exists to the east, southeast or south, since these will be preserved (by the adjacent 1), and therefore are simply artifacts of shrinking. The program is shown in figure 4.8.

The body of the program is a loop. The logic implements the conditions of the Levialdi shrinking operator and the disappearance test directly. At the bottom of the loop, the iteration is advanced, the condition to continue is tested and the count is accumulated.

The program exhibits important properties that enable the compiler to perform optimizations. Notice that all of the "at" references are to Im. The communication for these will be performed at the top of the loop. Once this communication is completed all of the computation in the first five lines of the loop are local. Additionally, the compiler will likely combine the two reductions. This is significant since for most parallel computers the cost of reduction is dominated by interprocessor communication, and since they can usually communicate two words for the same cost as communicating one, combining the two costs little more than a single reduction.

Notice that although the two reductions can generally be combined by the compiler to remove half of the communication overhead, the programmer could remove the reduction over Conn from the loop. Specifically, let Accum be an array of ubytes initialized to 0. Then, replacing line 39 by

```
Accum := Accum + Conn;
```

or its more succinct form

```
Accum += Conn;
```

the count of the components vanishing at a given position is kept. When the loop exits, the total can be computed by reducing Accum,

```
 1 program CountCon;      --                 Count Connected Components
 2 config var      n : integer = 512;        -- Image size in 1 dim.
 3 region          I = [1..n, 1..n];         -- Problem space
 4 var Im, Conn, Next : [I] ubyte;           -- Image arrays
 5
 6 direction    north  = [-1, 0]; NE = [-1, 1];
 7              east   = [ 0, 1]; SE = [ 1, 1];
 8              west   = [ 0,-1]; SW = [ 1,-1];
 9              south  = [ 1, 0]; NW = [-1,-1];
10
11 procedure CountCon();                      -- Entry point
12 var      smore : boolean;                  -- Loop control
13          count : integer;                  -- Num components
14          fptr  : file;                     -- UNIX file pointer
15          [I] begin                         -- Set boundaries to 0
16 [north of I]   Im := 0;                    --                     |
17   [NE of I]    Im := 0;                    --                     |
18 [east of I]    Im := 0;                    --                     |
19   [SE of I]    Im := 0;                    --                     |
18 [west of I]    Im := 0;                    --                     |
20   [SW of I]    Im := 0;                    --                     |
21 [south of I]   Im := 0;                    --                     |
22   [NW of I]    Im := 0;                    --                     V
23             count := 0;                    -- Initialize count
24             fptr := open("Image","r");     -- Find file
25             read(fptr, Im);                -- Get the image
26             repeat                         -- Over all I, iterate
27               Next := Im & (Im@north | Im@NW | Im@west);
28                                            -- Apply rules (a), (b)
29               Next := Next | (Im@west & Im@north & !Im);
30                                            -- Apply rules (c), (d)
31               Conn := Im@east | Im@SE | Im@south;
32                                            -- Find the 1's
33                                            --   preserving
34                                            --   connectedness
35               Conn := Im & !Next & !Conn;
36                                            -- Check disappearance
37               Im := Next;                  -- Advance iteration
38               smore := |<<Im;              -- Decide if continuing
39               count += +<<Conn;            -- Count all vanished
40                                            --   this time
41             until !smore;                  -- Stop when all zeroes
42             writeln(count);                -- Report results
43             close(fptr);                   -- Close up
44           end;
```

Figure 4.8
Connected components counting program using the Levialdi shrinking operator

```
writeln(+<<Accum);
```

eliminating the need for the variable `count` at the expense of adding the array `Accum`.

References

R. E. Cypher, J. L. C. Sanz and L. Snyder, 1990. "Algorithms for Image Component Labeling on SIMD Mesh Connected Computers," *IEEE Transactions on Computers,* 39(2):276–281.

5 Generalizing ZPL

In earlier chapters the basic array capabilities of ZPL were introduced. Many of those features have more advanced forms, which will be described in this chapter. The following specific topics will be treated.

Additional Region Specifications
Degenerate Ranges
@ Compositions
"At" In Region Specifiers
"Of" Compositions
"In" Regions
Combined Specifications

Dynamic Regions
Inheritance
Ditto

Indexed Arrays

Type Declarations

Flooding

Reduction/Scan Revisited

Region Conformance

Procedures
Declarations
Prototypes
Calls
Promotion
Recursion

Shattered Control Flow

Masks

Familiarity with the basic concepts from previous chapters is assumed.

Additional Region Specifications

There are a variety of simplifications that make defining regions easier.

Degenerate Ranges

In region specifications, a degenerate range, i.e., an index range of length 1, can be specified simply by giving that item. (One is the minimum length of any range of a dense region. See below.) Thus,

```
region Col1 = [1..n, 1..1];
```

is equivalent to

```
region Col1 = [1..n, 1];
```

The rule also applies for dynamic regions (see below).

@ Compositions

Multiple directions can be composed using @. For example, `A@east@north` has the same meaning as `A@northeast`, assuming the directions have their obvious definitions, `north=[-1,0]`, `east=[0,1]`, `northeast=[-1,1]`. The rule is that the resulting direction is found by adding the directions of the composition as vectors. Notice that because addition is commutative and associative, the resulting direction is the same regardless of the order of application, e.g., `A@north@east≡A@east@north`. Accordingly, no parenthesizing is necessary, nor is it allowed.

It is believed that a program's clarity is improved by declaring frequently used directions rather than repeatedly composing them. However, for occasional use compositions allow the direct formation of specialized regions from basic parts.

"At" in Region Specifiers

So far, @ has been used to translate arrays, but an analogous translation is also available for region specifiers using the letter sequence `at`. The symbols are restricted: the letter sequence `at` is used in the region specifiers only, while @ applies to array operands only. Thus, if `west = [0,-1]` and `R = [1..n, 1..n]`, then

```
[R  at  west]   . . .
```

specifies the region with a 0th column and no n^{th} column. And in

```
[R  at  west]  . . . A@east . . .
```

the `R` region of `A` is specified, assuming `east = [0,1]`. That is, the directions cancel. Cancelling directions are useful, as illustrated in the "move particles" code in chapter 9. Compositions are allowed with the region specifier form of `at`, e.g., `[R at east at north]` is allowed. Like @ compositions, the resultant direction is found by adding the directions as vectors. Parentheses are not necessary or allowed.

"of" Compositions

Multiple directions can be composed using of. For example, east of north of R is equivalent to northeast of R, assuming the directions have their obvious definitions given above. But the situation is more subtle than with the at. The rule for of computations is that the resulting region is found by evaluating the expression "inside-out," i.e., by applying the rightmost direction to the region, and then working out. Thus, the foregoing expression would be evaluated as if it were east of (north of R), although *parenthesizing is not permitted*. The inside-out rule for of compositions is natural: Since of is an operator taking both a direction and a region as operands and yielding a region as a result, applying the inside-out rule to an of composition effectively collapses *d* of *R* to *R'*, a new region, enabling the next outer most application of of.

Notice that because of-regions are disjoint from their base regions, expressions that would seem to "cancel," e.g., west of east of R, can be meaningful. So, assuming a 2D region R and the usual definitions for directions, the region west of east of R refers to the last column of R.

"In" Regions

The of operator constructs a border region that is adjacent to and just outside the edge of a base region. The in operator constructs a similar region just across the edge on the "inside" of the base region. That is, if R = [1..n, 1..n]

```
[east in R] . . .
```

refers to the last column of R, assuming east = [0, 1]. Also, assuming se = [1, 1]

```
[se in R] . . .
```

refers to the single element region { (n,n) } in the lower right corner of R. Notice that combinations of in are permitted *without parentheses,* allowing

```
[south in east in R] . . .
```

to be an alternative formulation for { (n,n) }. As with of, in combinations are evaluated inside-out from the base region.

Combination Specification

Two classes of combinations are permitted: in and of specifications can be mixed on the left hand side of a base region, and at can be simultaneously applied to a region that is constructed using in or of or a combination of the two.

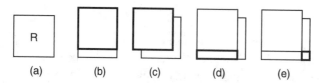

Figure 5.1
Combination of at and of. (a) Region R, (b) R at north, (c) R at north at west, (d) south of R at north at west, (e) east of south of R at north at west

To interpret a combination of in and of operators applied to a base region, evaluate them inside-out, just as with expressions composed exclusively of in or of.

For expressions containing at together with in or of, the region is found by applying the inside-out rule to the region as modified by the composed at's. Thus, if R is a rank 2 region

```
[east of south of R at north at west]
```

refers to the lower right corner index of R, since R at north at west shifts the array one position up and left, south of that region describes the last row shifted one position left, and east of that is the element to its right, i.e., the lower right corner. See figure 5.1. As previously mentioned, clarity is likely promoted by declaring frequently used regions rather than repeatedly specifying them using compositions.

Dynamic Regions

Regions, as explained so far, allow index sets to be named, i.e., declared, and to be formed by transformation using various prepositions. These are all static specifications of index sets in that once defined they are unchangeable. It is usually sensible to use statically known regions wherever possible, since a meaningful name can convey information to the programmer, there is less chance of error, and the compiler may be able to apply more optimizations in such cases. But there are computations that require an index set to vary, and for those cases dynamic regions are provided.

A dynamic region is not named, but is given literally within the region specifier of a statement. Typically, some of the lower or upper limit values will be computed. The index set defined by a dynamic region is computed each time the statement is executed, allowing the region to be different on each execution of the statement. For example, the assignment to A in

```
          for i := 1 to n do
[i, i..n]   A := 0;
          end;
```

has the cumulative effect of zeroing the diagonal and the upper triangle of A, assuming A is declared over region [1..n, 1..n]. The dynamic region specifies a rank 2 index set of shape 1×(n-i+1), where the value of the first index and the lower limit of the second index are different on each iteration. Thus, the assignment is applied to positions i through n of A's i^{th} row on the ith cycle through the loop. As a further example of a dynamic region,

```
[1..n, j..n]   pivot := max<<A;
```

limits the reduction to the last n-j+1 columns of A.

Dynamic regions are identical to static regions in every respect except that dynamic regions have their index sets recomputed each time they are encountered, and they cannot induce automatically allocated implicit storage, i.e., borders. They can greatly simplify programming, and should be used when needed, even though they are negligibly more expensive than static regions because of the repeated evaluation. Of course, they should be used where the capability they provide is not readily achieved by statically defined regions. Thus, one prefers the highly efficient

```
[R]    A := Index1;
```

to the less efficient text

```
          for i := 1 to n do
[i, 1..n]   A := i;
          end;
```

which is also probably a less transparent way to assign the elements of the ith row the value i.

The careful reader, recognizing that dynamic regions are given in square brackets and recalling that region specifiers on statements are also given in square brackets, might wonder why there are not two sets of brackets when the region specifier is a dynamic region? That is, if

```
[R]   A := ...;
```

is correct for static regions, why is

```
[1..n, 1..n] A := ...;
```

the equivalent dynamic region, instead of

```
[[1..n, 1..n]]  A := ...;
```

with its double brackets? Strictly speaking, the double brackets are correct, and this specification is allowed. However, it is also somewhat tedious to type the double brackets, so the ZPL compiler accepts either.

Simplified Region Specification

In addition to the simplifications of defining regions using prepositions shown above, there are two other very helpful facilities in ZPL, inheritance and dittoing.

Inheritance

To simplify specifying dynamic regions, it is possible to elide, or leave out, range specifications for any dimensions that are unchanged from the enclosing region. Those dimensions are said to *inherit* their ranges in those dimensions. Thus, for example, in the compound statement

```
[1..m, 1..n]begin
             ...
    [,2..n-1]  A := ...        -- First dimension inherits 1..m
             ...
            end;
```

the assignment to A is performed over the region [1..m, 2..n-1]. The second dimension, which differs from that of the enclosing region, must be given explicitly, but the first dimension, which is intended to be unchanged, need not be specified.

Ditto

Whereas inheritance allows a single dimension to be acquired from the enclosing region scope, the quote symbol ("), referred to as *ditto,* allows the whole applicable region to be referenced. One application of ditto is simply to save typing, as in

```
[1..m, i..n]begin
             ...
    [E of "]  A := ...        -- Refer to [1..m, n+1]
             ...
            end;
```

where it would have been necessary either to repeat the region `[1..m,1..n]` for the "of" expression, or to give the border explicitly, e.g., `[1..m, n+1]`. The direction with the ditto is thought to be better technique when there is no named region. (Notice that the rank of the applicable region is inferred by the way it is used, i.e., A is presumably, a rank 2 array and E is a 2D direction, so the ditto refers to the applicable rank 2 region.) Dittoes can be used wherever regions would be used in region specifiers. Thus `["  at south]` is another illustration of typical usage.

A second use of ditto is in implicit region references within procedures (see below). For example, suppose a procedure P is called within the scope of the 2D region R, i.e.,

```
[R]      X := P(...);         -- Call procedure P
```

Then, in the body of the procedure, it is possible to refer to R using the ditto notation. For example, within the procedure

```
[west in "] ...      -- Refer to first column
```

region expressions can use ditto and refer to the applicable region at the call site, in this case, R. See Procedures, below, for further information.

Indexed Arrays

ZPL has a second form of array, the indexed array. Syntactically, these look similar to arrays of scalar languages. The critical property for the ZPL programmer is that *indexed arrays are not a source of concurrency*. Unless used as components of parallel arrays (as described below), indexed arrays are replicated on each processor, and operations on indexed array values are repeated on each processor as scalar operations are. Nevertheless, indexed arrays are useful in many programming situations.

Indexed arrays are declared using the `array` keyword, followed by the range specifications for each dimension, followed by the keyword `of`, followed by a data type. (Notice that this use of `of` is unrelated to the `of` region operator from above.) The range specifications adhere to the same rules used for declaring regions. Thus,

```
var    ATMWGT : array [1..92] of float;
                                    -- Define 1D index array
       PIXMAP : array [1..8, 1..8] of ubyte;
                                    -- Define 2D index array
       LISTOLIST : array [1..10] of array [1..4] of integer;
                                    -- 1D array of 1D arrays
```

declares a variety of indexed arrays. Indexed array elements are referenced in the usual way by specifying the index of each dimension enclosed in square brackets. Thus,

```
. . . ATMWGT[30] . . .
. . . PIXMAP[1, 4] . . .
. . . LISTOLIST[4][3] . . .
```

illustrate references to specific items of the previously declared indexed arrays. As usual, expressions can appear in the brackets where constants are shown here.

References to indexed arrays must always be appended with index brackets. Also, some array operations from (parallel) arrays are available. These include the arithmetic and logical operators, and assignment. Array operations are signaled by specifying an empty index reference. Thus,

```
PIXMAP[] := PIXMAP[] + 1;   -- Array ops on indexed arrays OK
```

increments all elements of PIXMAP. For such expressions to be legal, only indexed arrays (or scalars) can be used on the right-hand side. Nor is it legal to apply reductions, scans, wrap, reflect, flood or permute operators.

It is possible to use indexed arrays as elements of parallel arrays, and vice versa. The resulting data structures are parallel. Thus, assuming R is a rank 2 region, then a 2D (parallel) array of 1D indexed arrays would be declared

```
var A : [R] array [1..10] of float;
                            -- 2D array of 1D indexed items
```

Every floating point number in the array can be initialized by

```
A[] := 0.0;      -- Initialize entire array
```

and individual positions can be treated as a unit, as in

```
A[10] := MAXFLOAT;        -- Set all last items to large
```

which sets the 10th element in *each* of the 1D arrays. Wrap and reflect apply, so

```
[west of R] reflect A[];      -- Mirror boundary
```

copies the indexed arrays, i.e., the 1D vectors, of the first column across to the western boundary.

Not only can indexed arrays be elements of parallel arrays, as just illustrated, but parallel arrays can be elements of indexed arrays. For example,

```
var  StateHist : array [1..3] of [R] float;
```

declares an indexed array whose elements are parallel arrays over [R] of floating point numbers, i.e., three parallel arrays. Reference to the parallel arrays is by indexing, e.g., StateHist[3]. The usual operations are applied in the usual way, e.g.,

```
        past := 1; pres := 2; futr := 3;
                                         -- Adopt names for states
        . . .
[R]     StateHist[past] := StateHist[pres];
                                         -- Make current state old
```

which assigns one parallel array to another. As always, the parallel array operations must be performed in the context of the appropriate region.

Of course, it is also possible to have an indexed array of parallel arrays whose items are themselves indexed arrays. However, no declaration can use more than one region specifier, i.e., only "one level" of parallel arrays is permitted. Since concurrency is expressed with parallel arrays, limiting the generalization in this way allows the concurrency to be focused at a particular site, namely, parallel arrays. There is no loss in expressive power, since both forms of array implement the array concepts.

Finally, when parallel arrays contain indexed arrays, it is possible to translate an operand with @ as well as to index it. In such cases the rule is: "the @ hugs the parallel array identifier". Thus,

```
... StateHist@east[pres] ...          -- @ hugs array
```

is correct, while

```
... StateHist[pres]@east ...          -- ILLEGAL subscript
```

is syntactically incorrect.

Type Declarations

Many quantities of interest in scientific computing are represented by multiple primitive values. Dates are composed of day, month and year, position is expressed by latitude, longitude and elevation, and orientation is given by roll, pitch and yaw. It is often convenient to refer to such composite quantities as whole units, while retaining the ability to use their constituent parts in computations. Such situations call for custom type declarations.

A type declaration is indicated by the keyword type, followed by an equal sign, followed by a type specification. So,

```
type triple = array [1..3] of uinteger;    -- Declare triples
```

declares a new type called a `triple` composed of a three element integer array. These types can then be used wherever the built-in types are allowed. For example,

```
var date, date_new, box_score : triple;
                                  -- Three valued variables
```

declares variables of the `triple` type. These variables can be manipulated as a whole

```
date_new[] := date[];        -- Assign all three fields
```

or as individual elements

```
date_new[2] := 1 + (date_new[2] % 12);       -- Advance month
```

The empty brackets are required, as usual for indexed arrays, when all elements are to be referenced.

An alternative to defining composite types by arrays is to define them as records. This is particularly useful when the constituent values are of different base types, or when symbolic names are particularly critical. So, for example,

```
type box_score = record
        runs  : ushortint;
        hits  : ushortint;
        errors: ubyte;
     end;
```

defines a type, `box_score`, composed of three integral fields. *Fields* are the constituents of a record. They are named, and within any record declaration the names must be unique. Note that the field types can be different.

The field names are used to refer to the values by means of the "dot" notation, in which the reference has the form `v.f` where `v` is a variable of the indicated type, and `f` is a field name of that type. So, for example given the declaration

```
var inning : box_score;
```

the value of the runs field can be referenced by `inning.runs`, as in

```
inning.runs := inning.runs + 1;       -- Another RBI
```

Since it is possible to have indexed arrays of defined types, the dot notation composes with indexing. So,

```
var GAME : array [1..2, 1..9] of box_score;
                              -- Declare indexed array
```

leads to references of the form GAME[2,7].runs. This can be contrasted with

```
type box_rows = record      -- Declare an alternate form
   runs  : array [1..9] of ushortint;
   hits  : array [1..9] of ushortint;
   errors: array [1..9] of ubyte;
end;
```

```
var GAMEa : array [1..2] of box_rows;
                              -- Declare GAME with alternate
```

in which the reference to the "runs in the bottom of the seventh" is now GAMEa[2].runs[7]. The field is an array, so the field reference, runs[7], requires an index. This is probably less intuitive than GAME[2,7].runs for the baseball context, but it is equivalent in storage.

Indexed arrays and records are often alternative ways of defining data types, but they present different advantages and disadvantages. On the one hand indexed arrays allow limited use of array operations, e.g., all values can be initialized at once, but all of the values must be of the same type. Records, on the other hand, can have values of differing types, but these values must be manipulated one item at a time. Clearly, both mechanisms are valuable tools for customizing a program's data representation to real world problems.

Flooding

One of the powerful features of ZPL is the ability to fill a matrix with copies of a row or a column, or more generally, to fill a higher dimensional array with copies of a lower dimensional array. This operation, called *flooding* in ZPL is a generalization of the idea of scalar promotion. In order to describe flooding, some basic vocabulary must be introduced:

floodable dimension—a dimension in a region specification in which the range is replaced by an asterisk. For example, the second dimension in the region specification [1..n, *] is a floodable dimension.

flood region—is a region defined with one or more floodable dimensions. For example, region F = [*, 1..n] is a flood region with a floodable first dimension.

flood array—is an array declared over a flood region. For example,

```
var Flrows, Flrose : [F] float
```

declares two flood arrays, assuming the F region from the previous definition.

The concept behind flooding is that the specified dimensions, i.e., the nonfloodable dimensions, define the size of the items that are replicated. The asterisk specifying a floodable dimension might be read as "an indeterminate number of," as in "the arrays Flrows and Flrose have an indeterminent number of n-item rows."

Flooding differs from the concepts introduced so far in that it requires two regions, the region defining the item to be replicated, and the region of the floodable array. The region of the flood array is simply the region "on the statement." The region of the array being replicated is given in brackets following the flood operator, >>. For example, the last row of the n × n matrix A can be flooded into the array Flrows by the statement

```
[F]   Flrows := >>[n,1..n] A;        -- Copy last row of A   (5.1)
```

yielding an array with an indeterminate number of identical rows. The region following the operator specifies the last row and the region applying to the whole statement gives the region of the result. Alternative forms of this flood statement would be

```
[F]   Flrows := >>[n,] A;            -- Copy last row of A
```

where the bounds of the second dimension are inherited, and

```
[F]   Flrows := >>[south in R] A    -- Copy last row of A
```

where an in specifies the final row. As another example, the statement

```
[F]   Flrose := >>[i,] B;            -- Flood row i of B
```

replicates row i of B into Flrose.

The two regions of a flood—the region of the replicated subarray, specified after the operator, and the region of the result, specified as the applicable region for the statement—must have the same rank. The array being replicated has to be "smaller," of course, in order to be replicated, but this is achieved by having "collapsed" dimensions, i.e., dimensions in which a specific index is given. In the above examples, the first dimension is collapsed. (See Region Conformance, below.)

As an example of flooding, consider the problem of determining if the last row of A is equal to any row of B. A temporary array, Flrows is filled with the last row of A, as in statement (5.1) above. This allows an element-wise comparison over B

```
[1..m,1..n] ... Flrows = B ...
```

that will yield an array with one or more rows filled with 1's if a match is found. See figure 5.2. (A partial reduction can be used to determine if a match exists; see below.) A flood array conforms to whatever number of items are required in the floodable dimension, so Flrows is treated as if it has m rows.

An important property of flooding is that only the defining data is stored in the representation of the flooded array, e.g., only the row defining Flrows in figure 5.2. This means that flood arrays get particularly good cache utilization as compared to fully represented arrays.

Reduction/Scan Revisited

Recall from chapter 3 the concept of a partial scan was introduced, i.e., a scan across a subset of the dimensions, allowing, for example, the "running sum" across each of the rows of an array to be computed. There is an analogous partial reduction formulated around the usual set of scan/reduce operations, +, *, max, etc. The principal complication to partial reduce is that it reduces a subset of the dimensions, producing a logically "smaller" array. Like flood, then, partial reduction requires that two regions be specified— the region of the operand and the region of the ("smaller") result. Like flood, a region is specified after the reduce operator to indicate a partial reduction.

So, for example,

```
[1..m,1] A := +<<[1..m,1..n] B;
                        -- Add B's columns, save in A's col 1
```

the region of the statement indicates that the first column is to be assigned. The region following the reduction operator is compared with the region on the statement. The difference in the second dimension indicates that the n columns reduce (by addition) to produce a single column, that is stored in the first column position of A. An alternate form of this statement might be

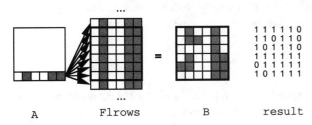

A	Flrows	B	result

Figure 5.2
The last row of array A is flooded into Flrows and compared to B to create the logical result array

```
[1..m,1] A := +<<[ ,1..n] B;
                              -- Add B's columns, save in A's col 1
```

where the column specification of the operator's region specifier is inherited, and

```
[west in R] A := +<<[R] B;
                              -- Add B's columns, save in A's col 1
```

where the first column is specified symbolically.

As another example, if A contains Pascal's triangle, its second dimension sum reduction results in the powers of 2,

```
1  0  0  0  0                              1
1  1  0  0  0                              2
1  2  1  0  0                              4
1  3  3  1  0                              8
1  4  6  4  1                             16

        A            [1..5,1]  ... +<<[1..5,1..5] A ...
```

Notice that the region to the right of the operator specifies the region for operations "preceding" the reduction, i.e., in computing the operand, while the region on the statement specifies the operations "after" the reduction. So, if R = [1..m,1..n], and south = [1,0], then in

```
[south in R]  A := (max<<[R](B+C))/Index2;
```

the sum of B and C is computed over the entire R region, since that operation is performed prior to the reduction, and so is determined by the right-hand side region. The reduce operates down columns, since [south in R] ≡ [m,1..n], implies a row result. The max of each of the columns forms the row that is divided by Index2, i.e., the integers 1 to n, and stored in the last row of A. The division and the assignment are both over the [south in R] region since they happen after the reduction.

It is a common programming idiom to partially reduce an array in one or more dimensions, and then replicate the result in these dimensions. For example,

```
[*, 1..n] Af1 := >>[1,] +<< [R] A;
                              -- Add up cols, replicate result
```

sums the columns into the first row, and then floods Af1 with the result. A curious aspect of the region requirements for flood and partial reduction is that some row, in this case 1, must be specified as a place to reduce to, and the place to flood from. This is arbitrary in that any row will do. Accordingly, specifying it is not necessary. Reducing into a flood array is sufficient to accomplish the flood, as in

```
[*, 1..n] Afl := +<<[R] A; -- Recommended way to add columns
                                      and replicate the result
```

which is conceptually cleaner, and is recommended.

Notice two points. First, although partial reduce and partial scan are related, the dimension over which the operation is performed is expressed differently—for scan it is given in brackets, while for reduce it is given by the "change" in the region between the operand and result.

```
[1..n, 1] ... +<<[R] A ...          -- Sum reduce rows
      [R] ... +||[2] A ...          -- Sum scan rows
```

This difference is a consequence of the fact that the reduce must specify two regions, while only one is needed for the scan. Second, neither operation changes the rank of the operand, i.e., the result has the same rank as the operand. So, in this example when the rows are summed up, the result is defined over a column region, i.e., a rank 2 region, as shown on the statement's region. This property motivates the topic of the next section.

As a closing observation, notice that there is a heuristic for remembering the operators reduce, scan and flood. In reduce (<<), the result is "smaller" than the operand, in scan (||) the result is the same size as the operand, and in flood (>>), the result is "larger" than the operand. In addition, scan is sometimes known as "parallel prefix."

Region Conformance

ZPL's operators have the property that their operands must be of the same rank, so that the selected values come from the same index set, possibly modified by an @. Thus, if A and B are declared over R = [1..n,1..n], then in

```
[R]      ... A + B ...
```

the addition refers to those elements of A and B with like indices from R. This is a strict rule. Thus, for example, if C is a rank three array declared over [1..c,1..n,1..n], it *might* seem reasonable to write

```
[R] [4,1..n,1..n] ... A + C ...    -- ILLEGAL mixing of ranks
```

but the application of binary operators to operands of different rank is not permitted.

A feature called *rank change* is planned for Advanced ZPL, which allows the rank of arrays to be changed to accommodate situations like the one just illustrated. However, even when the capability is available, programmers will achieve the best performance when they "work within the rank." This is because arrays are stored based on their ranks, and computing on operands of like rank assures that logically related values will be stored near one another, promoting efficiency. As will be seen, accommodating this requirement is not onerous.

The situations where "working within a rank" become relevant typically involve flooding, partial reductions, and, since they are often used to select a lower rank array, dynamic regions. Partial reductions provide a good example. Consider a 2D array A that is updated by some computation, and for which at the end of the iteration, the largest value in each row is compared to the largest on the last iteration. This computation is given by

```
[1..n, 1] BigNew := max<<[R] A; -- Find largest in each row
[1..n, 1] Ratio := BigNew/BigOld; -- Trend? >1 ==> increas'n
```

BigNew, BigOld and Ratio are logically one dimensional, but have been declared (elsewhere) to be "collapsed" 2D arrays, i.e., columns. This is because the partial reduce produces a single column result, determining BigNew. The "like rank" rule then forces BigOld and Ratio to conform.

Procedures

ZPL provides the usual procedure mechanism, including recursion. As with other languages, procedures in ZPL are a powerful structuring mechanism making a program easier to write, understand and maintain. But, procedures are also a convenient mechanism for specifying concurrency through the use of promotion. This section covers procedure declarations, prototypes, calls, promotion and recursion.

Procedure Declarations

Procedures are declared anywhere after the program statement, though it is conventional to declare them following the config var, constant, direction, region, type and var declarations, since these are typically global information applicable to all procedures, implying they should be specified first. The general form of a procedure declaration is

```
procedure PName ({Formals}) { : Type}
   {Locals}
   Statement;
```

where the non-italicized items must be given literally, the italicized items must be replaced
with text of the indicated type, and the items in braces are optional. *PName* is a user
specified procedure identifier. *Type* gives the type of the procedure's result, i.e., the type
of the value `returned` for functions. *Locals* is an optional set of local-to-the-procedure
variable declarations, which come into existence when the procedure is entered and are
discarded when the procedure is exited. *Statement* is a single statement performing the
computation, called the procedure body. This is usually, but not always, a `begin-end`
compound statement. For example, an exceptional case would be

```
procedure absolute(x: float) : float;
   if  x ≥ 0.0
      then return x
      else return -x
   end;
```

a value returning procedure, i.e., a function, computing the absolute value of its argument.
Since the `if`-statement is a single statement, no `begin-end` is required to enclose it.

The (possibly empty) *Formals* list gives the procedure's formal parameters, separated
by semicolons, i.e., the names of the arguments to be used in the procedure's definition.*
A single list item typically declares a sequence of parameters of a single type according
to the following scheme:

{ `var` } *Id_List* : *Type*

where the non-italicized items must be given literally, the italicized items must be replaced
with text of the indicated type, and the braces indicate an optional item. The *Id_List* is a
subsequence of the procedure's parameters, all of the same *Type*. For example,

```
procedure squarefloor( x, y : float; var xf, yf : integer);
   begin
      xf := floor (x * x);
      yf := floor (y * y);
   end;
```

---

* Notice that the required parentheses explain why the program procedure, i.e. the procedure with the program's
name which typically has no arguments, is always specified with empty parentheses.

has four parameters, two of which are `floats`, and two of which are `integers`. Further, the last two parameters are "by-reference" parameters, discussed momentarily.

If a formal parameter is an array, its characteristics must also be specified analogously to its original declaration, as in

```
procedure even_up ( Odds : [R] integer) : [R] integer;
    return Odds - Odds % 2;
```

Such a specification requires that the arrays passed to the procedure be declared over R, but it does not require the computation be performed over all of R. Rather, the region over which the computation is performed will be inherited from the call site, because no region specifier is given in the procedure. Thus, for example, the procedure Compress0s, to shift a row of an array left z positions,

```
procedure Compress0s( var z : integer; var Row : [R] float);
    while z > 0 do
      begin
          Row := Row@east;
          z := z-1;
      end;
```

has no region specifier in it. So, when it is called in a loop,

```
          for i := 1 to m do
                    j := amt;           -- The amt of shift is j
[i, 1..n]  Compress0s(j, A); -- Shift row i of A by j
          end
```

the region specifying the row to be shifted is inherited from the site of the call. That is, on the ith call to Compress0s, the region applying to the statement Row := Row@east will be [i, 1..n].

Another way for a procedure to accept arrays as parameters is by the *rank defined* mechanism. A rank defined specification gives only brackets and possibly commas. These imply the argument's structure and allow the flexibility of arguments defined over different regions. Thus for example,

```
procedure Twice (X : [,] float) : [,]float;
    return 2.0 * X;
```

the X array is rank defined. All arguments passed to Twice must be rank 2, and their dimensions will be inherited. The applicable region will be whatever the applicable rank 2 region is at the call site. Thus, in

```
[1..2, 1..2] A := Twice(B);
```

a 2×2 region of B is doubled, while in

```
[1..n,1] A := Twice(B);
```

the first column is doubled.

The rank of the parameter must be inferable from the rank of the array specification. This is trivial when the region is given literally,

```
procedure P0(X : [R] float);
                         -- X is a parallel array over region R
```

and straightforward for rank defined arrays.

```
procedure P1(X : [,] float);   -- X is a parallel array of
                               -- rank 2 that inherits its
                               -- region specification from
                               -- the call site
```

It is not possible to infer the rank from a ditto specification, however, since the procedure might be called from sites where different ranks prevail. So,

```
procedure P2(X: ["] float);        -- ILLEGAL use of ditto
```

is illegal. Finally, passing an indexed array

```
procedure P3(X : array[1..n] of float);
                                  -- X is an Indexed array
```

requires the array declaration to be given explicitly in the procedure specification.

Parameters can be passed to a procedure by either of two methods, as *by-value parameters* or as *by-reference parameters*. The procedure header indicates which form is being used: The keyword var indicates that the names following are by-reference parameters; otherwise, they are by-value parameters. As a heuristic var means that the procedure can only be called with variables in corresponding parameter positions.

In the case of value parameters the actual parameter's value (from the procedure call site) is copied "into" the formal parameter variable of the procedure. All references to this parameter within the procedure refer to the local copy. Modifications to by-value parameters change only the local copy. When the procedure exits, the copy is discarded. Consequently, any assignments to the local copy will be lost.

For by-reference parameters, i.e., var parameters, no copy is made. Rather, all references to the formal parameter within the procedure simply refer to the variable that is the actual parameter value from the call. Modifications to the formal parameter will change the actual parameter. Thus, by-reference parameters are a secondary means of returning results to the caller, as shown in the `squarefloor` procedure above. The main purpose of by-reference parameters is to save copying large parameters such as arrays and large records into the procedure. Wherever possible, `var` parameters should be used for this benefit.

Procedure Prototypes

It is essential that a procedure be declared before it is used. But, if in procedure P there is a call to procedure Q, and within procedure Q there is a call to P, how can the declare-before-use rule be respected? The solution is the *procedure prototype,* which is simply a completely specified procedure header in which the keyword `prototype` replaces the keyword `procedure`. For example,

```
prototype absolute(x: float) : float;
```

is a prototype for the absolute procedure from above. Notice that all information about the parameter types and return value are given as in the declaration. The prototype simply "stands in" for the declaration prior to the actual declaration. Thus, the sequence

```
prototype Q ( var x, y : float): float;
                                    -- State basics of Q's call
procedure P ( var u, v : float); -- Declare procedure P
   . . .
procedure Q ( var x, y : float): float;
                                    -- Declare procedure Q
   . . .
```

gives a prototype for procedure Q so that it can be called (in procedure P) prior to its declaration. All parts of the procedure header must be given in both places and *be identical.*

Procedure Call

A procedure is called, or *invoked,* by giving its name and supplying the parameters. If the procedure is a value returning procedure then it may be invoked in an expression as if it were an identifier. Thus

```
change := change + absolute(segment); --Accumulate magnitude
```

invokes the `absolute` procedure declared above. If the procedure is not value returning, it is invoked as a statement and must appear alone, followed by a semicolon. Thus, the `squarefloor` procedure, given above, is treated as a statement

```
squarefloor(xbase+deltax, ybase+deltay, xlimit, ylimit);
```

since it is not value returning. It returns its results by changing its last two parameters. Notice that the (actual) parameters supplied in the procedure call can be variables or expressions if the corresponding parameter is declared as a by-value parameter. But if the parameter is declared as a by-reference parameter using `var`, then the actual parameters in the call can only be variables. Thus, in the `squarefloor` procedure call just illustrated, expressions can be used in the first two parameter positions only.

Promotion

Sequential procedures are procedures that use no array constructs, i.e., do not contain parallel array declarations, region specifiers, uses of parallel arrays, `wrap`, `reflect`, flooding, mask, reduce or scan. They also cannot call non-sequential procedures. The `absolute` and `squarefloor` procedures defined above are sequential procedures. Sequential procedures can be promoted to apply to arrays. That is, their scalar (formal) parameters can be bound to array (actual) parameters in a call, to give the effect of applying the procedure to each item of the arrays. For example,

```
[R] A := absolute(A);        -- Remove negative
```

applies the sequential procedure to items of the array A over the region R.

Promotion of sequential procedures is a convenient (and an efficient) way to perform complex operations in parallel on arrays. See chapter 9 for examples.

Recursion

A procedure that calls itself, or calls a procedure sequence that ultimately results in a call to itself, is said to be *recursive*. ZPL procedures can be recursive. (See figure 5.3.)

Shattered Control-flow

ZPL programs that use scalars in control-flow expressions, such as

```
if n%2 = 0  then       -- Check if problem size is even
        ...
```

have a single, sequential thread of control, i.e., one statement is executed at a time. Specifically, in the statement forms

```
if lexpression then statements { else statements } end;
```

Procedure Declaration and Call Check List

A parameter's type must be declared, as well as the ranks of any arrays.

Value parameters keep a local-to-the-procedure copy.

With no local copy, be-reference parameters, i.e., `var` parameters, refer indirectly to the actual parameters.

Any changes in a procedure to value parameters are lost on exit.

Any changes in a procedure to reference parameters persist on exit.

Value parameters can be passed as an identifier or an expression.

Only identifiers can be passed as by-reference parameters.

Figure 5.3
Procedure Usage Check List

if *lexpression* then *statements*
        {{elsif *lexpression* then *statements*}}
        {else *statements*} end;
for *var* := *low* to *high* { by *step* } do *statements* end;
while *lexpression* do *statements* end;
repeat *statements* until *lexpression*;

when the *lexpression*s, *var, low, high* and *step* are scalar values, there is only one statement executing at any time.

It is permissible to use parallel arrays in the *lexpression*s, *var, low, high* and *step* positions of these control-flow expressions, subject to certain restrictions. Parallel arrays used for any of these values are said to cause the control-flow to *shatter*. In shattered control-flow, each index value has its own thread of control. When the statement list execution is completed, the control-flow returns to sequential execution. The limitations are as follows:

Restrictions on shattered control-flow: The statement list forming *statements* cannot assign to scalar variables. A variable modified by @ must be identical in all instances. Uses of `wrap`, `reflect`, flooding, permutation, reduction, scan, mask and region specifiers are prohibited.

The restrictions ensure that when the control-flow shatters, the computation performed at each index value is based on values that are "known" to that index. The intuition behind the restriction is that when the control-flow shatters, there is no guarantee what computation is taking place at other index positions, and so operations that reference other index positions, e.g., wrapping, may not be meaningful.

Though shattered control-flow may seem curious, it simply allows operations to be written in the body of the program that could be realized by writing a scalar function and promoting it. For example, to compute factorial of each element of an array without shattered control flow, a scalar factorial procedure would be defined,

```
procedure fact(n: integer): integer;
begin
  var product, i: integer;
  product := 1;
  for i := 2 to n do
  product := product*i;
  end;
  return product;
end;
```

and then applied to a (parallel) array of non-negative integers by promotion,

```
A := fact(B);
```

to realize the result.

With shattering the factorial computation can be realized by the code,

```
A := 1;                 -- Initialize, so 0! is 1 and 1! is 1
for I := 2 to B do
   A := A*I;            -- Compute the factorial of B
end;
```

assuming that I is declared as an array. The index variable of the for-loop is the array I, and the loop limit is the array B. This is more direct and more succinct than the promoted function solution.

It is generally believed that using procedures is a good programming technique, since they encourage code reuse, encapsulate common processing logic, promote abstraction, etc. But writing procedures for operations just for promotion when they could easily be placed in-line in the program causes unnecessary proliferation of procedures. Shattered control-flow allows for in-line program text to behave like the application of a promoted scalar procedure. Notice that if the factorial computation were required multiple times in a program, the explicit use of a promoted function would become the preferred solution, since it is about as efficient, names the operation and reduces the chance of making a notational error in writing the code.

The most common application of shattering is to perform different computations on different array elements based on an `if` test. Thus,

```
if A >= 0
   then
     B := sqrt(A);
   else
     B := sqrt(-A);
end;
```

which is an effective way to realize selective execution. Masks are another alternative.

Masks

ZPL makes it trivial to operate uniformly on all elements of arrays, and it is nearly as simple to operate selectively on arbitrary subsets of regions. The mechanism is called a *mask,* and it is expressed as a modifier in a region specifier. Thus, in the sequence

```
         M := A > 0;    -- Boolean array, 1's at positive
                        -- positions
[R with M]    B := sqrt(A); -- Take square roots of positive
                        -- items
```

M is an array of 1s and 0s indicating the truth value of the test. In the second line, M is used as a mask. It specifies that the statement is to be applied only to those indices of the region where M is nonzero, i.e., logically true. The forms of masking are,

```
[R with M]
[R without M]
```

where R is any region specifier including ditto, and M is a `boolean`, `ubyte` or `sbyte`. The `without` operator is the opposite of `with`, i.e., the statement is applied to index values corresponding to zeroes, i.e., logical false.

Masking, like all region specifiers used with statements, are scoped. Thus, a mask applies to all of the statements within its scope. When masks are cascaded, i.e., a masked statement appears in a sequence of statements already masked, the inner mask supersedes the outer mask(s). Thus, if

```
M1 ≡ 1 0 1 0 1 0  and  M2 ≡ 1 1 1 0 0 0 .
```

then

```
[V]              X := 1;       -- X ≡ 1  1  1  1  1  1
[V with M1]      begin
                    X:=X+1;    -- X ≡ 2  1  2  1  2  1
    [V with M2]     X:=0;      -- X ≡ 0  0  0  1  2  1
[V without M2]      X:=4;      -- X ≡ 0  0  0  4  4  4
                 end;
```

has the affect of applying operations within the `begin-end` compound statement to the odd index positions. Within the compound statement, that application is superseded by M2 and its complement.

Finally, a mask can be changed within the scope in which it is applicable, but the change is not manifest until after the completion of execution of the scope. Thus, in

```
[" with M1] begin
            S1;
            M1 := M1@west;
            S3;
          end;
```

the changes to M1 will not apply until the next execution of the `begin-end` statement.

Though the restrictions on shattered control-flow prohibit the use of masks, these can generally be performed prior to the shattering. For example,

```
            A := 1;               -- Initialize
            M := B >= 0;          -- Find nonnegatives
[R with M]  for I := 2 to B do    -- Mask outside the loop
                A := A*I;         -- Factorial
            end;
```

computes the factorial on only nonnegative values using masking. Since the mask is applied to the statement, rather than to a statement in the body of the shattered loop, it is legal.

6 Programming Techniques

The power of ZPL derives largely from the fact that computations are expressed by manipulating whole arrays rather than by manipulating individual scalar values, as in Fortran or C. There are several advantages: The programming is simpler when less detail is required, making the program easier to write in the first place and easier to understand later when it must be changed. Also, arrays in ZPL express the computation in a simple, succinct way that is more likely to be analyzed successfully by the compiler than is intricate scalar logic. When the compiler "understands" the program, it can produce highly efficient code customized to the target computer. Thus, the computations can actually be more efficient when expressed as arrays.

Though the examples in previous chapters have all been quite natural and obvious, programming with arrays may be sufficiently new to many programmers that a discussion of principles and further illustrations of "standard" array techniques should be useful. Accordingly, this chapter works through a series of computations solved using whole arrays:

Computation	Constructs Illustrated
Matrix Multiplication	
Cannon's Algorithm	Wrapping, dynamic regions
SUMMA	Flooding
Sparse Matrix Product	Indexed arrays
Ranking	Partial reductions
Histogramming, revisited	Flooding, Partial reductions
Vector Quantization Data Compression	Indexed arrays
Odd/Even Transposition Sort	Masking

The emphasis will be on using the new techniques introduced in the last chapter, and illustrating good style. (To reduce detail, the "whole program" aspects of the examples such as including I/O will be dispensed with, since these are illustrated in chapter 4.)

Matrix Multiplication

As mentioned in chapter 1, finding the product of an $m \times n$ matrix $\mathbf{A}$ and an $n \times p$ matrix $\mathbf{B}$ producing an $m \times p$ matrix $\mathbf{C}$ is usually written in a scalar language as a triply nested loop:

FORTRAN MM   C MM

```
      DO 10 J = 1,M                    for (i=0;i<m;i++){
        DO 10 I = 1,P                    for (j=0;j<p;j++){
          C(I,J) = 0                       c[i][j]=0;
          DO 10 K = 1,N                    for (k=0;k<n;k++){
 10   C(I,J)=C(I,J)+A(I,K)*B(K,J)            c[i][j]=c[i][j]
                                                a[i][k]*b[k][j];
                                           }
                                         }
                                       }
```

This specification is too rigid for effective use on high performance computers, since it specifies how to produce the result in a strict one-operation-at-a-time order. It states that $c_{1,1}$ is to be produced before $c_{1,2}$, and that in producing each $c_{i,j}$, the product $a_{i,1}b_{1,j}$ is to be produced before $a_{i,2}b_{2,j}$, which in turn is to be computed before $a_{i,3}b_{3,j}$, etc. But, it is not necessary to follow this rigid order to produce the result. All of the $c_{i,j}$ values can be computed independently in any order or in parallel, all of the $a_{i,k}b_{k,j}$ multiplications of each dot product could be computed simultaneously, and even the addition of these k subproducts to form $c_{i,j}$ can be performed with considerable concurrency. Some compilers attempt to figure out that such rigid sequencing is not strictly necessary, and since matrix multiplication is an intensively studied example, they are frequently, but not always successful on this computation [Ngo 97]. In general, however, computations are much more complex, compilers fail to eliminate the unnecessary sequentiality, and the resulting object programs have very limited concurrency. Thus, when a computation does not require a specific order of execution, it is preferable not to specify one. This is the concept behind ZPL's array operations. The compiler is more likely to produce efficient object code when irrelevant constraints are not imposed by the programmer.

From these considerations a guideline emerges for formulating effective algorithms for ZPL programs. Since the operations in each statement of a ZPL program apply independently to all indices of the region, a useful rule is:

Maximize the size of the regions over which each statement applies.

This will result in a maximum number of independent operations for which the compiler can plan fast execution. Even when a ZPL program is not executed on a parallel machine, the rule will often aid the compiler in improving performance of the cache, instruction pipeline, etc. A corollary to the rule is suggested by previous discussions:

Minimize the use of intricate control-flow.

Since the control-flow enforces a specific order of execution, the more involved it becomes, the less likely it is that a compiler will be successful in finding optimizations. Of course, both guidelines must be applied with judgment.

How should matrix product be expressed in accordance with these guidelines? There are several ways to compute matrix product in ZPL, and two are considered here to illustrate computational ideas that are further discussed later.

Cannon's Algorithm   A well known approach that leads to a clean ZPL solution is Cannon's algorithm [Cannon 69, Kung & Leiserson 80]. To explain the approach, visualize the computation (figure 6.1) as taking place in space. The result matrix **C**, initialized to 0.0, remains in a fixed position while skewed instances of the **A** and **B** matrices are logically "passed over" **C** at right angles. As elements of **A** and **B** "pass over" a result position, they are multiplied together and added into that result position. Thus, on the first step the value $a_{4,1}b_{1,3}$ is added to $c_{4,3}$. On the second step both arrays advance so that $a_{4,2}b_{2,3}$ is added into $c_{4,3}$; additionally, $a_{3,1}b_{1,3}$ is added into $c_{3,3}$, and $a_{4,1}b_{1,2}$ is added into $c_{4,2}$. And so forth. The process completes when the **A** and **B** matrices have completely passed over **C**.

At the mid-point in the computation multiplication and addition operations are taking place at every position in the result array, a property that is consistent with globally maximizing the independent operations. Towards improving the concurrency of the earlier and later steps, where not all positions are participating, notice that the matrices can be given in a more normal rectangular orientation by wrapping the skewed portions from the front of the representation to the back in the case of A and from the top to the bottom for B. See figure 6.2.

```
c11 c12 c13                     a11 a12 a13 a14
c21 c22 c23    ⇐            a21 a22 a23 a24
c31 c32 c33               a31 a32 a33 a34
c41 c42 c43          a41 a42 a43 a44
        ⇑

        b13
     b12 b23
  b11 b22 b33
  b21 b32 b43
  b31 b42
  b41
```

Figure 6.1
Cannon's matrix product

```
c11 c12 c13          a11 a12 a13 a14|
c21 c22 c23          a22 a23 a24|a21
c31 c32 c33          a33 a34|a31 a32
c41 c42 c43          a44|a41 a42 a43

                          ⇐

b11 b22 b33      ⇑
b21 b32 b43|
b31 b42|b13
b41|b12 b23
```

Figure 6.2
Packing the skewed arrays into rectangular form for the revised algorithm

The lines show the boundary between the end of the skewed array and the "wrapped" portion. The principal effect of removing the skewing is that for the computation to be correct, the two operand arrays must begin in a superimposed position "above" **C**, and as the computation proceeds, their values must circulate by wrapping around in the direction of the arrows so that the operand pairs of the subcomputations align. For example, in the $c_{3,3}$ position $a_{3,1}$ of the **A** matrix is multiplied by $b_{1,3}$ in the **B** matrix on the first step. See figure 6.2. If **A** is shifted-and-wrapped left on each step, and **B** is shifted-and-wrapped up on each step, the property that subcomputations of $c_{i,j}$ are performed at the i,j position will hold. The key feature of this reformulation is that at each step computation is taking place at all positions in the result array, i.e., over its whole region, which achieves the goal of maximizing the region over which the computation is performed. The entire ZPL program to implement the Cannon matrix multiplication solution is shown in figure 6.3.

The first step is to formulate the declarations, beginning with the appropriate regions

```
region     Lop  = [1..m, 1..n];   -- Left operand shape
           Rop  = [1..n, 1..p];   -- Right operand shape
           Res  = [1..m, 1..p];   -- Result shape
```

which would collapse to a single region if the matrices were square. Although the shifting will be left for A and up for B, it will be more convenient, as explained below, if the directions point in the direction from which the operands will come.

```
direction     right = [ 0, 1]; below = [ 1, 0];
```

The remaining declarations

```
var     A: [Lop] float;        -- Left operand matrix
        B: [Rop] float;        -- Right operand matrix
```

```
 1 region       Lop   = [1..m, 1..n];    -- Left operand shape
 2              Rop   = [1..n, 1..p];    -- Right operand shape
 3              Res   = [1..m, 1..p];    -- Result shape
 4
 5 direction    right = [ 0, 1]; below = [ 1, 0];
 6
 7 var          A: [Lop] float;          -- Left operand matrix
 8              B: [Rop] float;          -- Right operand matrix
 9              C: [Res] float;          -- Result matrix
10              i: integer;              -- Iteration variable

12                      for i := 2 to m do     -- Skew A
13 [right of Lop]         wrap A;              --   Move 1st col beyond last
14    [i..m, 1..n]        A := A@right;        --   Shift last i rows left
15                      end;
16
17                      for i := 2 to p do     -- Skew B
18 [below of Rop]         wrap B;              --   Move 1st row below last
19    [1..n, i..p]        B := B@below;        --   Shift last i cols up
20                      end;
21
22              [Res] C := 0.0;                -- Initialize C
23
24                      for i := 1 to n do     -- For A&B's common dimension
25              [Res]     C := C + A*B ;        -- Form product and accumulate

26 [right of Lop]       wrap A;                -- Send first col right
27          [Lop]       A := A@right;          -- Shift array left
28 [below of Rop]       wrap B;                -- Send top row down
29          [Rop]       B := B@below;          -- Shift array up
30                      end;
```

Figure 6.3
Cannon's Matrix Multiplication

```
        C: [Res] float;      -- Result matrix
        i: integer;          -- Iteration variable
```

define the variables of the computation.

The first step is to skew the arrays in place. No skewing is required for the first row of A. The second row of A needs to be shifted left and wrapped one position, the third row must be shifted and wrapped around two positions, etc. The skewing will be performed iteratively, such that on the ith step, rows $i + 1$ through m are wrapped and shifted one position. A dynamic region limits the shifting to rows i through m.

```
              for i := 2 to m do  -- Skew A
[right of Lop]    wrap A;         --   Move 1st col beyond last
   [i..m, 1..n]   A := A@right;   --   Shift last i rows left
            end;
```

The effect of the `wrap` statement is to copy into the column to the `right` of the `Lop` region of A, the column on the opposite side of the array, i.e., the first column. Then, when A is replaced with itself offset to the `right`, the result is to shift the array left. The results of the three iterations needed to skew A of the previous example are shown in figure 6.4. The logic

```
                for i := 2 to p do   -- Skew B
[below of Rop]    wrap B;            --  Move 1st row below last
   [1..n, i..p]   B := B@below;      --  Shift last i cols up
                end;
```

for skewing B vertically is analogous. The final preparatory step is to initialize the result array C.

Now, for as many items as there are in the common dimension, i.e., n, A is multiplied by B and accumulated into C over the [Res] region, and the entire operand arrays are cyclically shifted one position on each iteration.

```
                 for i := 1 to n do -- For A&B's common dimension
         [Res]   C := C + A*B;      -- Form product and accumulate
[right of Lop]   wrap A;            -- Send first col right
         [Lop]   A := A@right;      -- Shift array left
[below of Rop]   wrap B;            -- Send top row down
         [Rop]   B := B@below;      -- Shift array up
               end;
```

Notice that unlike the initial skewing of the operand arrays, the wrapping in the main loop involves all elements of both operands.

One property of this solution is that it leaves the operand arrays in the compact-skewed position. If they are required in their proper form later, they must be "unskewed." If so, it is preferable to begin by copying the arrays to temporaries which are used in the computation. These can be discarded rather than unskewed when the computation is completed. Notice that the C array is oriented in its proper position. Finally, this solution accumulates the results in an order different than is given in the sequential algorithm shown at the start of this section. The solution is equivalent for real numbers, of course, but not necessarily identical in the finite precision of floating point computer arithmetic.

SUMMA Algorithm   Another solution that is especially easy to program in ZPL is the Scalable Universal Matrix Multiplication Algorithm of van de Geijn and Watts [97]. In ZPL this algorithm can exploit the power of flooding for the data communication. The

```
a11 a12 a13 a14│ −        a11 a12 a13 a14│a11
a21 a22 a23 a24│ −        a22 a23 a24 a21│a21
a31 a32 a33 a34│ −        a32 a33 a34 a31│a31
a41 a42 a43 a44│ −        a42 a43 a44 a41│a41
        Initial                  i=2 step


a11 a12 a13 a14│a11       a11 a12 a13 a14│a11
a22 a23 a24 a21│a22       a22 a23 a24 a21│a22
a33 a34 a31 a32│a32       a33 a34 a31 a32│a33
a43 a44 a41 a42│a42       a44 a41 a42 a43│a43
        i=3 step          i=4 step
```

Figure 6.4
Intermediate values at the bottom of the loop while skewing A

result is a highly efficient program. To simplify the presentation, assume $m \times n$, i.e., the matrices are square.

To explain the SUMMA algorithm, recall that every item c_{ij} in the matrix product result is the sum of the products of row i of **A** times column j of **B**. The first of these terms is $a_{i,1}b_{1,j}$. The SUMMA solution computes all of these first terms simultaneously. This can be accomplished by flooding the first column of **A** and the first row of **B** into flood arrays, and multiplying corresponding elements:

$$
\begin{matrix}
a_{11} & a_{11} & a_{11} & a_{11} \\
a_{21} & a_{21} & a_{21} & a_{21} \\
a_{31} & a_{31} & a_{31} & a_{31} \\
a_{41} & a_{41} & a_{41} & a_{41}
\end{matrix}
\quad \times \quad
\begin{matrix}
b_{11} & b_{12} & b_{13} & b_{14} \\
b_{11} & b_{12} & b_{13} & b_{14} \\
b_{11} & b_{12} & b_{13} & b_{14} \\
b_{11} & b_{12} & b_{13} & b_{14}
\end{matrix}
\quad = \quad
\begin{matrix}
a_{11}b_{11} & a_{11}b_{12} & a_{11}b_{13} & a_{11}b_{14} \\
a_{21}b_{11} & a_{21}b_{12} & a_{21}b_{13} & a_{21}b_{14} \\
a_{31}b_{11} & a_{31}b_{12} & a_{31}b_{13} & a_{31}b_{14} \\
a_{41}b_{11} & a_{41}b_{12} & a_{41}b_{13} & a_{41}b_{14}
\end{matrix}
$$

Flood **A**'s 1st column   Flood **B**'s 1st row   Result elements accumulated into **C**

The second term can be computed analogously, by flooding the second column of **A** and the second row of **B**. The algorithm continues in this fashion, so that on the kth iteration the kth term of the dot product is computed and accumulated into the result array, **C**.

Notice that although each item in the result is computed by combining an A row times a B column, to compute all of the entries simultaneously, we flood an A *column* and a B *row*. This may seem backwards, but as one can readily recognize, it allows the "matching" index positions to align. The easily specified ZPL program for the SUMMA algorithm is shown in figure 6.5. The program begins by declaring the necessary regions, including flood regions (lines 2–3), and the appropriate variables. After initializing the result array C (line 9), an iteration proceeds to compute each term of the dot product by

```
 1 region M  = [1..n, 1..n];      -- Region for n x n dense matrix
 2        Fc = [1..n, *];          -- Flood region for left operand
 3        Fr = [*, 1..n];          -- Flood region for right operand
 4 var A,B,C : [M] double;         -- Operand and result matrices
 5        Af : [Fc] double;        -- Flood array for left operand
 6        Bf : [Fr] double;        -- Flood array for right operand
 7        k  : integer;            -- Iteration index
          . . .
 9          [M]  C := 0.0;         -- Initialize
10               for k := 1 to n do
11          [Fc]    Af := >>[1..n,k] A; -- Replicate kth column of A
12          [Fr]    Bf := >>[k,1..n] B; -- Replicate kth row of B
13          [M]     C  := C + Af*Bf;-- Compute kth term in dot prod.
14               end;
```

Figure 6.5
Flood-based matrix multiplication solution

flooding columns of A into Af, flooding rows of B into Bf, and multiplying and accumulating the intermediate products (lines 11–13).

This program is about the simplest possible solution for multiplying dense matrices in ZPL,* even simpler than the straightforward Cannon algorithm. This is a happy outcome, because these algorithms use techniques exploited in the fastest parallel matrix multiplication algorithms running on present day parallel computers. This suggests that a critical ZPL design goal—that its facilities should tend naturally to lead programmers to effective solutions—has been achieved in this instance at least.

As a postscript to this exercise programmers are reminded that matrix product is a common and expensive operation. Accordingly, vendors generally supply a matrix product subroutine that is customized to their hardware. Such routines will generally run faster than a program written in a high level language, though the ZPL flooding solution has outperformed library routines. The programs given here are convenient, and will suffice for all but the most intensive applications of matrix product. For these extreme cases a call to such a library routine is generally advised.

Sparse Matrix Product

The matrices that arise in many scientific computations have the property that they are sparse, i.e., only a few of the entries are nonzero. Representing such matrices as dense

---

* Flooding can be used to replicate the 2D arrays A and B into 3D to be multiplied together elementwise. The result is produced with a partial sum-reduction. This 1-line matrix multiply, though still time and space efficient, is not as space efficient as the row-column version presented here.

matrices with all of the zeroes given explicitly is very wasteful of both space and time. So, these matrices are generally represented in compact form where only the nonzero values are stored. A typical compact form would represent each row by pairs of values, the first item of which is the column index for the nonzero matrix entry, and the second item is its value. Thus, if row 50 had nonzeroes in columns 49, 50, 51 and 52 then

```
(49, 2.0) (50, 4.0) (51, 6.0) (52, 8.0)
```

would be its compact representation.

As an illustration of computing with compact representations, consider a sparse matrix multiplication computation. To simplify matters, only the special case of tridiagonal matrices will be considered, that is, matrices in which the nonzeroes of row i are in columns $i - 1$, i and $i + 1$. Since all of the nonzeroes are in regular positions, storing the column numbers with the values is unnecessary. The values are stored in a linear array, where each entry is a triple representing a row, such that the $i - 1$st item is stored in the first position, followed by the ith and $i + 1$st items. Accordingly, the array

```
1 2
1 2 3
  2 3 4
    3 4 5
      4 5 6
        5 6 7
          6 7
```

would appear as

```
0 1 2
1 2 3
2 3 4
3 4 5
4 5 6
5 6 7
6 7 0
```

In order that the diagonal (ith) element always to be in the second position, it is necessary to begin the first row in the second position. As will be seen later it is convenient if the first element is assigned 0. Similarly, padding the last row with a 0 will make the algorithm work out nicely.

This approach implies the following declarations

```
region  R = [1..n];
type  cform = array [1..3] of float;
var A, B, C : [R] cform;
```

for the compact form data representation. Notice the region is one dimensional.

   To formulate the matrix multiplication algorithm, focus on the elements of, say, the 4th row. Of the items in the resulting matrix, **C**, only three entries will be nonzero, $c_{4,3}$, $c_{4,4}$ and $c_{4,5}$, and of the terms in their defining equations,

$$\cdot \quad \cdot \quad \cdot$$

```
c43 ≡ a41b13+a42b23+a43b33+a44b43+a45b53+a46b63+a47b73
c44 ≡ a41b14+a42b24+a43b34+a44b44+a45b54+a46b64+a47b74
c45 ≡ a41b15+a42b25+a43b35+a44b45+a45b55+a46b65+a47b75
```

$$\cdot \quad \cdot \quad \cdot$$

only the elements shown in bold are nonzero. This simplifies the computation. For example, given that all three arrays are represented in the same compact form, it is necessary only to refer to values in the rows above and below a given row, e.g., to compute row 4, only rows 3 and 5 need be referenced. This motivates the definition of two directions,

```
direction above = [-1]; below = [+1];
```

to allow the previous and next rows to be referenced.

   The computation of the product is direct by generalizing the equations given above. The three values for a row, `C[1]`, `C[2]` and `C[3]`, are computed simultaneously by the equations

```
C[1] := A[1]*B[2]@above+A[2]*B[1];                -- i-1
C[2] := A[1]*B[3]@above+A[2]*B[2]+A[3]*B[1]@below; -- i
C[3] :=                 A[2]*B[3]+A[3]*B[2]@below; -- i+1
```

Recalling that the indexes 1, 2 and 3 correspond to column indices $i - 1$, i and $i + 1$, the value of the diagonal element `C[2]` is computed by multiplying the three values stored in an A row times the three B values found by selecting the last value from the row `above`, the diagonal of the present row and the first value in the row `below`. The other two elements are similarly computed. The three statements compute all elements of the result matrix simultaneously, provided there is suitable initialization: First, the 0th and $n + 1^{st}$ rows of B must be initialized to 0.0 so that the `above` and `below` references are defined and vanish when computing the terms for the first and last rows, respectively. This motivates the initialization

```
 1 region    R = [1..n];                              -- Only 1D Region needed

 2 type  cform = array [1..3] of float;               -- Create compact form
 3 var A, B, C : [R] cform;                           -- Matrices are compact
 4 direction above = [-1]; below = [+1];              -- Refer as rows
              ...
 6          [R] begin
 7 [above of R]    B[]  := 0.0;                        -- Initialize 0th row
 8 [below of R]    B[]  := 0.0;                        -- Initialize n+1st row
 9                 C[1] := A[1]*B[2]@above + A[2]*B[1];
10                 C[2] := A[1]*B[3]@above + A[2]*B[2] + A[3]*B[1]@below;

11                 C[3] :=                   A[2]*B[3] + A[3]*B[2]@below;

12              end;
```

Figure 6.6
Tridiagonal matrix multiplication using compact form

```
[above of R] B[] := 0.0;
[below of R] B[] := 0.0;
```

By leaving the brackets empty, the assignment is to each element of the triple. Second, to assure that the C[1] entry for row 1 and the C[3] entry for row n compute to zero, B[1] of row 1 and B[3] of row n must be initialized to 0.0 as well. Since this is the normal way to represent the array, the requirement is treated simply as a property of the input, rather than a value to be computed. The result is shown in figure 6.6.

Ranking

Ranking a set of items is a common operation. It is easily performed in ZPL. For the example here, assume that the n items to be ranked come from some small finite set of values such as the integers 1 to s. There will be duplicates, since $s \ll n$, and the rule is that when values are the same, the one with the lower index in the input is to have the lower rank.

The technique is to use an $s \times n$ temporary array P to represent the position of the item. See figure 6.7. P is set to 0s and 1s such that there is a 1 in position i,j if item j has value i; and 0s elsewhere. These settings are computed by flooding the input into the rows of an array and comparing that to the row index, Index1. By adding up these 1s (with a scan) and removing the intermediates (by multiplying by P), the columns of P can be reduced to yield the result. A program fragment is shown in figure 6.8.

Several features of the program are significant. First, the source array (In) and output array (Out), which are logically one dimensional arrays, are defined to be single-row two dimensional arrays. This is because the computation will operate in two dimensions, and

Input (s=3): 3 1 1 2 1 3   Output: 5 1 2 4 3 6

Flood Input	Index1	P	+||P	P*(+||P)	Reduce Cols
3 1 1 2 1 3	1 1 1 1 1 1	0 1 1 0 1 0	0 1 2 2 3 3	0 1 2 0 3 0	5 1 2 4 3 6
3 1 1 2 1 3	2 2 2 2 2 2	0 0 0 1 0 0	3 3 3 4 4 4	0 0 0 4 0 0	
3 1 1 2 1 3	3 3 3 3 3 3	1 0 0 0 0 1	5 5 5 5 5 6	5 0 0 0 0 6	

Figure 6.7
Ranking $n=6$ items ranging over $s=3$ values

```
 1 region  Io = [1, 1..n];          -- Region for the input/output
 2         R  = [1..s, 1..n];        -- Basic working region
 3         F  = [*, 1..n];           -- Flood region
 4 var In,Out : [Io] ubyte;          -- Problem is limited to 256 < s
 5         P  : [R];                 -- Processing array
 6         Z  : [F];                 -- Flood array
     . . .
 8    [F]  Z := >>[Io]In;            -- Replicate the input
 9    [R]  P := Z = Index1;          -- Mark where there are items?
10    [R]  P := P * (+||P);          -- Find the overall order
11    [Io] Out := +<<[R] P;          -- Add up columns w/partial reduce
```

Figure 6.8
Ranking computation based on scan and partial reduction

it is highly efficient to work "within the same rank," as explained in the discussion on Region Conformance in the last chapter.

Second, the computation relies on the fact that the plus-scan wraps around on each row as it accumulates the entries of an array.

Third, the partial reduce that adds up the columns must specify which dimension is being reduced. This is expressed by the "difference" between the region of the statement [Io] and the region following the operator [R]. Specifically, the region on line 11 is [1,1..n], while the region specified with the reduction is [1..s,1..n], implying that the first dimension reduces.

Finally, the computation may appear very "heavy weight," but in fact it is likely to be quite efficient. As mentioned in the flooding definition, flood arrays are represented with only the defining values. So, Z is not 2D despite being used that way. Index1 is a logical array created by the compiler, and does not occupy memory. The scan operation will be implemented by the efficient parallel prefix technique, as will the reduction. Finally, though ZPL relies on the native C compiler for low level optimizations, many compilers perform "strength reduction" optimizations on operations such as the multiply by 0–1 values here, i.e., an equivalent sequence of operations not involving multiply may be used. And even when the compiler doesn't perform strength reduction, it is likely that the multiply is a better choice than an if-then-else on modern pipelined processors.

Thus, this ranking solution is likely to be reasonably efficient even ignoring the benefits of parallel processing.

Histogramming, Revisited

In chapter 4 a small histogramming program was presented, which printed the ranges of the intervals and the number of items assigned to each interval. Using the ideas from the ranking example above, it is possible to consider an alternative implementation based on the partial reduce operation. See figure 6.9.

This solution begins by revising the previous 1D region to a 2D, single row region. The logic follows the earlier solution, computing bin numbers by dividing each item by the interval size, correcting to 1-origin. The histogramming operation comes in the final step where the BinNo array is flooded in the first dimension, i.e., the rows are replicated, and then compared to Index1 to create a logical array that is accumulated row-wise to form the result. The size of the flooded intermediate array comes from the region specified with the partial reduction, i.e., [1..b,1..n]. The partial reduce is performed across the second dimension, as can be seen by inspecting the region of the partial reduction operator and the region of the context (line 14).

Revisit the example from the chapter 4 histogram program, in which b ≡ 3 and the input

```
1 region   Rw = [1,1..n];        -- The index space of the data
2 var small, big, size : float;  -- Real scalars
3    Hist  : [1..b,1] integer;   -- Array to hold histogram
4    Values: [S] float;          -- Data value array
5    BinNo : [S] ubyte;          -- Interval no., expect at most 255
    . . .
7 [S]begin
8    small  := min<<Values;      -- Find a smallest value
9    big    := max<<Values;      -- Find a largest value
10   size   := (big-small)/b;    -- Figure size of the intervals
11   BinNo  := ceil((Values-small)/size);-- Compute position, round
up
12   BinNo  := BinNo + !BinNo;   --Include small endpoints in first
13                               -- bin yielding 1-origin indexing
14 [1..b,1] Hist := +<<[1..b,1..n](Index1 = >>[1,1..n] BinNo);
15                               -- Flood BinNo down columns, compare
16                               --    to create logical rows to sum
17                               --    over to find histogram directly
18     end;
```

Figure 6.9
Revised histogram computation

```
1 1 1 1 1 1 1 1      3 1 2 2 3 1 1 1      0 1 0 0 0 1 1 1           4
2 2 2 2 2 2 2 2      3 1 2 2 3 1 1 1      0 0 1 1 0 0 0 0           2
3 3 3 3 3 3 3 3      3 1 2 2 3 1 1 1      1 0 0 0 1 0 0 0           2
        (a)                  (b)                  (c)             (d)
```

Figure 6.10
Values from line 14 of the Histogram program of figure 6.9: (a) `Index1`, (b) `>>[1,1..n] BinNo`,
(c) `Index1 = >>[1,1..n] BinNo`, (d) `Hist`

Values ≡ 6.3 -4.2 0.0 1.9 5.4 -2.2 -4.2 -2.2

resulted in bin numbers

BinNo ≡ 3 1 2 2 3 1 1 1

Then line 14 produces the result 4 2 2 and the intermediate values shown in figure 6.10.
This is effectively the same solution as presented before, except that it is performed as
a single operation rather than iteratively. And, like the ranking solution, should be efficient
for moderate values of b.

Vector Quantization Data Compression

The bits of an image are often compressed so that, for example, they can be transmitted
efficiently over a low bandwidth communication link. There are lossless compression
schemes that allow all bits of the image to be reconstructed later, and lossy compression
schemes that lose some information in order to achieve a much greater degree of
compression. Lossy schemes are chosen when the use made of the images is not materially
affected by the lost information. Vector quantization is one such lossy scheme.

In vector quantization a codebook is created by "training" it on a sample set of images.
This codebook is then used to compress/decompress the images. In the ZPL program
shown here, the 8-bit pixels of an image are considered to be arranged in 2×2 groups
which are matched against the 2×2 pixel entries of a 256-entry codebook and replaced
by the index of that codebook entry that most closely matches. Thus, this lossy scheme
achieves a 4:1 compression ratio. The 2×2 groups motivate the definition of a data type,
`block`, which is a 2×2 indexed array. The images (`Im`) and the codebook (`CB`) have
blocks as items. The simple program is shown in figure 6.11.

The program begins with the declarations, all of which are by now standard, except
for the data type declaration `block`. The variable `Im` represents an image as `blocks`,
so that its default size in `blocks`, 512×512, implies an image of 1024×1024 size in
pixels.

A function dist(b1, b2) is defined to take two blocks as parameters and return the floating point number that is the mean square distance between them. Since the blocks are 2D indexed arrays, the computation simply makes explicit reference to the items of the blocks, and returns the result. The procedure is a scalar procedure in the sense that it takes single items of type block as parameters, though these elements are themselves arrays, of course. When the dist procedure is used in the body of the program, it will be called with a scalar first argument, a block from the codebook, and an array second argument, the image. This causes the procedure to be promoted to apply to each position, i.e., each block of the image.

The program begins by reading in the codebook CB which, to avoid being distracted by the details of I/O, is not shown. Then, in the processing loop images are read in, compressed, and the compressed results are written out. The logic of the processing loop is particularly simple. The "old" distance array, Disto, is initialized to be the distance of every image block to the first codebook entry. Then, for the remaining entries in CB, the "new" distance to every image block Distn is computed, and the best so far is stored in the Coding array. When all codebook entries have been considered, the contents of Coding is the compressed image, which is written out. Notice that the update of the best match (lines 30–34) is performed using shattered control flow. That is, the condition of the if-statement

```
Disto > Distn
```

is a test over arrays, so the statement is executed independently for every index in the region, R. For those in which the best previously computed distance, Disto, is larger than the new distance, Distn, the new distance is saved and its index stored in Coding. For those indices for which the condition does not hold, there is no change.

The Compress computation is highly efficient. Since the codebook array, CB, is an indexed array it is replicated on each processor when the program is executed in parallel. This means that each processor of a parallel computer can perform its part of the compression without any interprocessor communication. This makes the core of the program maximally concurrent. The key issue in the program's performance concerns the details of reading in the raw images and writing out compressed images. Parallel I/O is crucial, but unfortunately it is a very machine specific operation. So, it is not possible to evaluate the performance of this computation fully.

Odd/Even Transposition Sort

Ordering a set of elements is a computation with wide application, and one that has been intensively studied. Since it is generally possible to sort much faster when one exploits

```
 1 config var n : integer = 512;      -- Image size
 2 region      R = [1..n, 1..n];      -- Problem domain
 3 type    block = array [1..2, 1..2] of ubyte;
 4                                     -- The compression is based on
 5                                     -- 2x2 blocks of 8-bit pixels
 6 var CB: array [0..255] of block;    -- Codebook, an indexed array
 7     Im: [R] block;                  -- Image array
 8  Disto,                             -- Old distance array
 9  Distn: [R] float;                  -- New distance array
10 Coding: [R] ubyte;                  -- Coding array
11      i: integer;                    -- Loop index
12
13 procedure dist(b1, b2: block): float;
14    -- A function to compute the mean square distance
15    -- Block b2 to be promoted
16    return ( (b1[1,1] - b2[1,1])^2
17           + (b1[1,2] - b2[1,2])^2
18           + (b1[2,1] - b2[2,1])^2
19           + (b1[2,2] - b2[2,2])^2)/4.0;
        . . .
21 -- Input codebook here
22 [R] repeat                          -- Compress all images ...
23       -- Input an image blocked into Im
24       Disto := dist(CB[0],Im);      -- Init old distance array
25       Coding := 0;                  -- 1 is closest so far
26
27       /* Move through codebook, finding how they match up */
28       for i := 1 to 255 do
29         Distn := dist(CB[i],Im);    -- Compute distance for entry
30         if Disto > Distn            -- Shatter to process entries
31           then
32               Disto := Distn;       -- New distance is smaller
33               Coding := i;          -- ith entry is best so far
34           end;
35         end;
36       -- Output the compressed image in Coding
37    until no_more;
```

Figure 6.11
Lossy data compression program

the specifics of a particular computer, vendors typically provide a highly optimized sorting procedure customized to their hardware. When the data set is very large, or sorting is used repeatedly, it is advisable to invoke the library procedure, rather than a sort written in ZPL or any high level language. Nevertheless, sorting provides a handy illustration of several language features.

The Odd/Even Transposition Sort orders a linear array of items by comparing each odd indexed item with the next element, and interchanging them if they are out of order. This operation applied to all odd-even pairs is called a half step, and clearly, since the data items do not interfere, the operations can be performed simultaneously. The other half step is to perform the same operation on each even-odd pair. The sort repeatedly applies the two half steps until no interchanges take place, i.e., every element is in order with respect to its successor.

A ZPL program for the masking version of the computation is shown in figure 6.12. The program begins with standard declarations. It then sets up a constant array, Oe, which has 1's in alternating positions (line 12). The logic of the program after initializations is to iterate (lines 19–36), performing the two half steps until there is no change, i.e., unordered (line 34) is false. If the array is initially sorted, the loop is never entered, due to the initial assignment (line 16) of unordered.

Of interest is the use of masking to restrict attention first to the out-of-order odd-even pairs (lines 22–25), and then the out-of-order even-odd pairs (lines 29–32). In line 22, Mask is true for odd indexed values that are larger than the following element, and it is only for these values that the array operations within the begin-end statement will have an effect. Accordingly, if Mask is true for index i, the ith element of Temp is assigned the smaller value, and the $i + 1^{st}$ element of Temp is assigned the larger value of the pair. Notice that each index value is considered for each statement, and so the execution time is not significantly affected by how many Mask bits are set. To assist in understanding the execution of OET_Sort, these intermediate values of Mask and Val for n=8

Line 21.5		Line 28.5	
Mask	Val	Mask	Val
1 0 1 0 0 0 0 0	3 1 4 1 5 9 2 6	0 1 0 0 0 1 0 0	1 3 1 4 5 9 2 6
0 0 0 0 1 0 1 0	1 1 3 4 5 2 9 6	0 0 0 1 0 0 0 0	1 1 3 4 2 5 6 9
0 0 1 0 0 0 0 0	1 1 2 3 4 5 6 9	0 0 0 0 0 0 0 0	1 1 2 3 4 5 6 9

```
 1 program OET_Sort;                          -- Odd/Even Transposition Sort

 2
 3 config var   n : integer = 100;            -- Problem size
 4 region       V = [1..n];                   -- Problem Space
 5 direction next = [1];                       -- Reference to right neighbor

 6
 7 procedure OET_Sort();                       -- Entry point
 8 var      Val, Temp   : [V] float;           -- Value arrays
 9          Mask, Oe    : [V] ubyte;           -- Arrays to mark interch's
10          unordered   : boolean;             -- Termination condition
11          [V] begin
12                Oe := Index1%2;              -- Set alternate positions
13                read(Val);                   -- Get input
14    [next of V]  Val := max_float;           -- Disable final element
15                Mask := Val > Val@next;      -- nonzeroes indicate disorder

16                unordered := |<<Mask;        -- Is there disorder?
17                Temp := Val;                 -- Initialize
18
19                while unordered do
20                  /*  Odd Halfstep */
21                  Mask := Mask & Oe;         -- Mark odd unordered items
22    [" with Mask]  begin                     -- Wherever these occur
23                    Temp := Val@next;        -- Set larger
24                    Temp@next := Val;        -- Set smaller
25                  end;
26                  Val := Temp;               -- Update
27                  /*  Even Halfstep */
28                  Mask := (Val>Val@next) & !Oe;-- Consider evens
29    [" with Mask]  begin                     -- Wherever disorder exists
30                    Temp := Val@next;        -- Set larger
31                    Temp@next := Val;        -- Set smaller
32                  end;
33                  Mask := Val > Val@next;--Where disorder remains
34                  unordered := |<<Mask;      -- Any change?
35                  Val := Temp;               -- Update
36                end;
37                writeln(Val);                -- Print it
38              end;
```

Figure 6.12
Odd/even transposition sort

were produced by inserting write statements before the masked compound statements, i.e., at lines 21.5 and 28.5.

References

L. F. Cannon, 1969, "A Cellular Computer to Implement the (Kalman) Filter Algorithm," Ph.D. thesis, Montana State University.

H. T. Kung and C. E. Leiserson, 1980, "Algorithms for VLSI Processor Arrays," In Carver Mead and Lynn Conway (eds.), Introduction to VLSI Systems, Addison-Wesley.

Ton Ahn Ngo, 1997, The Role of Performance Models in Parallel Programming Languages, Ph.D. dissertation, University of Washington.

Robert van de Geijn and Jerrell Watts, 1997, "SUMMA: Scalable universal matrix multiplication algorithm," Concurrency Practice and Experience, 9(4):255–274.

7 Advanced ZPL Concepts

In previous chapters fundamental ZPL concepts such as regions, directions, translations, etc. have been introduced. In this chapter, generalizations to those concepts are introduced that allow much more sophisticated programs.

Strided Regions and Arrays

In addition to working with dense arrays, ZPL programmers also have the ability to compute over arrays in which elements have been uniformly "removed." The regions and arrays are called *strided,* because skipping indices at regular intervals between referencing elements is suggestive of "walking" over the index ranges with "long strides." Strided arrays are the way in which multigrid and wavelet computations are expressed in ZPL.

As with other features of ZPL, striding is accomplished through the use of regions. To "stride" a region, the key word `by` is used with a direction, as in

```
region S = [0..9, 0..9] by [ 2, 2];
```

which has the effect of defining S to have only even number indices in both dimensions. That is, beginning with a region in brackets with 100 index pairs, the definition of S yields a region with only 25 index pairs.

$$S = \{(0,0), (0,2), (0,4),\dots,$$
$$(2,0), (2,2), (2,4),\dots, (8,8)\}$$

In effect, the direction gives the stride for each dimension, i.e., the amount to be added to an index in each dimension to find the next index.

Strided regions are usually defined from a base region. Thus,

```
region  R = [0..n-1, 0..n-1];
        S = R by [ 2, 2];
```

defines R and then defines S as a strided by `[2,2]` variant of R. Notice that the index sets of R and S are related in that S contains alternate index positions of R. Of course, it is possible to make multiple regions, as in

```
region  R  = [0..n-1, 0..n-1];
        S2 = R by [ 2, 2];
        S4 = R by [ 4, 4];      -- Recommended style
        S8 = R by [ 8, 8];
```

which could also be defined successively, as in

```
region  R  = [0..n-1, 0..n-1];
        S2 = R  by [ 2, 2];
```

```
S4 = S2 by [ 2, 2];        -- Alternate form
S8 = S4 by [ 2, 2];
```

In general, it is thought to be better programming style to define all strides relative to the base region, i.e., the first form is preferred. Some ZPL programmers find it convenient to use indices in the base range 0..n-1 rather than the range 1..n in order to make it easy to express which items are present in a strided region, e.g., "indices divisible by 4".*

It is not necessary to stride in all dimensions. To declare a region with dense indices in the first dimension, but alternate indices in the second dimension, i.e., stride the rows, write

```
region  Sr = R by [ 1, 2];      -- Stride rows by 2
```

Similarly, a three dimensional region with only the first dimension strided might be declared

```
region  S3D = [0..r, 0..s, 0..t] by [2, 1, 1];
```

Of course, the stride amount must be a positive integral value. Notice the useful heuristic that the direction gives the dimensions of the bounding box of the subarray that is "collapsed" into each strided index.

Strided regions can be used wherever dense regions can be used. As with other region specifications it is possible to stride regions dynamically. Thus

```
[[0..i-1] by [2]] ...;

                       -- Reference alternate elements up to i
```

defines a one dimensional dynamic strided region, where the value of i is bound when the statement is executed.

Arrays with strided indices are declared in the usual way using strided regions. Thus, assuming the declarations given above,

```
var By2Pos: [S2] double; -- Strided array with even indices
    By4Pos: [S4] double; -- Strided array with indices
                         -- divided by 4
```

---

* Some multigrid programmers think of the indices of the coarser grids as dense, i.e., as stepping by a unit stride. ZPL does not provide the ability to remap strided indices into dense sequences, preferring instead to preserve the correspondence between present elements of any stride. But, if 0-origin indexing is used, then it is easy to mentally remap the indices to dense positions, since strided region indices always have the stride as a factor, assisting mental remapping. Thus, for example, index 12 would correspond to index 6 in a dense remapping of a strided-by-2 dimension, while it would correspond to index 3 for a dense remapping of a strided-by-4 region.

```
    By8Pos: [S8] double; -- Strided array with indices
                         -- divided by 8
```

defines arrays with the index sets indicated.

Recall that in chapter 3, the following rule was introduced:

Any array can be used in the scope of any region specifier provided the array is defined for all indices specified in the region.

In chapter 3 the rule prevented the use of arrays whose index sets were smaller than the regions in whose scope they were used. In the context of strided arrays, the rule means that computations must be performed in the scope of region specifiers that are aligned and have the same or larger strides. Thus, assuming the declarations from above,

```
[S2]   By2Pos := 0;        -- Initialize strided region
```

is the proper way to reference a strided region, but

```
[R]    By2Pos := 0;        -- ILLEGAL
```

is illegal because R contains index pairs that By2Pos does not have. The rule prohibits this kind of usage.

Of course, it is quite appropriate for an array to have more elements than are referred to in the strided region. So, assuming the declarations

```
region R = [0..n-1, 0..n-1];   S2   = [R] by [2,2];
var   X : [R] double;          Xby2 : [S2] double;
```

a possible way to aggregate the elements of X into Xby2 would be expressed

```
[S2]   Xby2 := 0.4*X + 0.25*X@east + 0.25*X@south + 0.1*X@se;
```

where the region is strided, as is the left-hand side array, but the array, X, is dense. The elements of X that are referenced in the subexpression $0.4*X$ are those of the region S2. The X@east expression in the scope of S2 means that the elements of X with an odd index in the second position are to be referenced. That is, the direction east = [0,1] is added to each of the indices of the strided region as usual to produce a new index set with which to reference X. Similarly for X@south and X@se. Of course, border regions may be required on the right and bottom to assure that all references are defined, e.g., when n is odd.

As just discussed when the array is dense, directions define neighbors in the usual way even if the region providing the index set happens to be strided. When the array is strided, directions also define neighbors in the usual way, but now there is a subtlety. What is the east neighbor of a strided-by-2 dimension? In the dense case the east neighbor can be computed by adding 1 in that dimension, i.e., by adding the stride, and in the strided-by-2 case the east neighbor is also found by adding 2, the stride.

Consider a strided-by-2 linear array Alt,

```
var Alt  : [0..n-1]  by [2] double;
```

whose values are to be linearly interpolated to fill a dense array Full. The direction right2 = [2] is used to reference the next element in the strided region in the statement sequence

```
[[0..n-1] by right2] begin
                        Full := Alt;                -- Set evens
                        Full@right := (Alt+Alt@right2)/2.0;
                                                    -- Set odds
                end;
```

where right = [1] refers to the next among the dense indices, and there is assumed to be a border element of Alt with index n.

An alternative way to have expressed the same computation would have been to refer to the two strided subsequences of [0..n] separately, and to use left = [-1] to reference the previous element, as in

```
[[0..n-1] by right2]  Full := Alt;                -- Set evens
[[1..n] by right2]    Full := (Alt@left + Alt@right)/2.0;
                                                  -- Set odds
```

Though Alt is not defined for any of the indices in [[1..n] by right2], the fact that each instance of Alt in the second line is modified by a direction that produces only indices of defined values fulfills the requirements of the previously mentioned rule.

In summary, the neighboring elements of a strided array can be referred to using @d, but it is essential that when direction d is added to the indices of the applicable region that they refer to defined elements of the array. This will generally mean that the neighbor referenced with direction d in a dense array will have to be scaled by the stride to perform the same reference in the strided array.

Multidirections

Strided regions often present situations in which it is convenient to "compute" directions, i.e., the specific neighbor to be referenced is a variable rather than a constant. Much of the flexibility of fully computed directions can be achieved by using multidirections.

A multidirection is a regular sequence of directions with a common name. The elements of the sequence can be referenced by name and index. The general form is to declare the multidirection as follows

```
direction Dname{ index set } = direction scaledby expression;
```

where

Dname is an identifier naming the direction

index set is a nonnegative lower and upper limit separated by ..

direction is any direction, i.e., integer d-tuple

expression is any arithmetic expression containing instances of the symbol { } in operand positions

and all other symbols must be given as shown. For example, assuming the 1D direction `right = [1]` the multidirection declaration

```
direction stride_right {0..5} = right scaledby 2^{};
```

defines the sequence of six directions,

```
stride_right{0}  ≡  [1] * 2^0 ≡  [1]
stride_right{1}  ≡  [1] * 2^1 ≡  [2]
stride_right{2}  ≡  [1] * 2^2 ≡  [4]
stride_right{3}  ≡  [1] * 2^3 ≡  [8]
stride_right{4}  ≡  [1] * 2^4 ≡  [16]
stride_right{5}  ≡  [1] * 2^5 ≡  [32]
```

of varying distances to the right. The multiple directions are defined relative to a base direction, in this case `right`, by scaling with the *expression*. The brace pair { } stands for multidirection indices such that the ith index i replaces the brace pair in the expression.

Like all directions multidirections are referenced using the standard @ symbol with operands except that an index is also specified in braces, { }. Thus, for example, assuming the `stride_right` directions declared above,

```
for i := 0 to 5 do
    ... A@stride_right{i} ...
end;
```

has the effect of referencing items of A shifted right one position for $i = 0$, then two positions for $i = 1$, etc., up to 32 positions to the right for $i = 5$.

In the multidirection declaration the lower and upper limits of the index interval are arbitrary expressions evaluating to nonnegative integer constants (lower ≤ upper). The base direction can be any legal direction. The scaling expression can be any expression involving instances of a brace pair, {} in operand positions and evaluating to an integer. For each index in the range the expression is evaluated with that index value substituted for all occurrences of {}, and the result is multiplied times each dimension of the base direction to yield the direction for that index.

As a further illustration, assuming se = [1, 1], the

```
direction SE{1..4} = se scaledby {};
```

defines the four directions

```
SE{1} ≡ [1,1] * 1 ≡ [1,1]
SE{2} ≡ [1,1] * 2 ≡ [2,2]
SE{3} ≡ [1,1] * 3 ≡ [3,3]
SE{4} ≡ [1,1] * 4 ≡ [4,4]
```

which point to the four consecutive elements below and to the right of a given element. Another application for multidirections is restructuring a dense array into a strided array of arrays. Given the declarations

```
region V = [0..3*n-1];
var D : [V]  float;                     -- Dense array of 3n items
    S : [V by 3] array [0..2] of float;
                                        -- Sparse array of triples
direction r{0..2} = [1] scaled by {};
                                        -- Pt to self, next, next+1
```

the multidirection r is composed of the three directions [0], [1] and [2]. Then, in the loop

```
[V by 3] for i := 0 to 2 do
             S[i] := D@r{i};           -- Fill elements of S
         end;
```

the strided array S is loaded from D. (See figure 7.1.) That is, the dynamic region, with indices {0, 3, 6, . . . } references all and only the items of S, and each element of S, a 3-element array, is loaded with the corresponding three successive elements of D, as the figure illustrates. Such restructuring has many applications.

First Iteration: `[R] S[0] := D@r{0};  -- Same as S[0] := D`

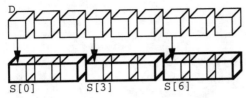

Figure 7.1
Loading sparse-indexed vector of triples from dense array using a multidirection

Multiregions and Arrays

Hierarchically structured data and algorithms are common in computing. For example, multigrids are formed from dense grids by striding at multiple levels. Wavelets are another example. The number of levels is determined by the size of the input, and therefore cannot be determined before program execution time. Accordingly, the concept of a multiregion is essential for defining and computing on an arbitrarily deep hierarchy.

In the same way that directions are extended to be indexable, so too, are regions. The general syntax for a multiregion is:

`region` *Rname* `{} =` *region* `by` *direction* `{} ;`

where

Rname is an identifier naming the region

region is any dense region

direction is any multidirection name followed by empty braces

and all other symbols must be given as shown. That is, multiregions are the same as other strided regions, except that the direction is a multidirection. For example,

```
direction sepow2{0..log2(n)} = [1,1] scaledby 2^{};
                                        -- By powers of 2
```

defines for $n \equiv 16$ the directions

```
sepow2{0} ≡ [ 1, 1]
sepow2{1} ≡ [ 2, 2]
sepow2{2} ≡ [ 4, 4]
sepow2{3} ≡ [ 8, 8]
sepow2{4} ≡ [16,16]
```

The region specification

```
region H{} = [0..n-1, 0..n-1] by sepow{};
                                    -- Hierarchical region
```

therefore, defines for $n \equiv 16$ a five level hierarchy

```
H{0} ≡ {(0,0), (0,1), (0,2), . . . , (15,15)}
H{1} ≡ {(0,0), (0,2), (0,4), . . . , (14,14)}
H{2} ≡ {(0,0), (0,4), (0,8), . . . , (12,12)}
H{3} ≡ {(0,0), (0,8), (8,0), ( 8, 8)}
H{4} ≡ {(0,0)}
```

in which the 0th level is a 16x16 dense region, the 1st level is an 8x8 region strided by [2,2], the 2nd level is a 4x4 region strided by [4,4], the 3rd is a 2x2 region strided by [8,8], and the 4th is a 1x1 region with a single index value. Clearly, when $n \equiv 64$ the R region is a seven level hierarchy, etc.

As suggested in the example, multiregions are referred to by appending a brace pair containing the index of the level being referenced. For example,

```
[H{3}]   X := Y;        -- Update X
```

has the effect of updating four elements of X, assuming the declaration above. In general, an indexed multiregion can be used wherever standard regions can be used.

Since regions are used to declare arrays, it follows that declaring an array with a multiregion must produce a multiarray. Multiarrays are declared using a multiregion with empty braces with the region specifier, as in

```
var     G{} : [H{}] double;        -- Declare multiarray G
```

and they are referenced by appending braces with an index, as in G{1}. The semantics simply extend the normal meaning of array. That is, the identifier, G in this case, refers to an array with index positions corresponding to each index in the multiregion. This can be thought of as array levels corresponding to each level in the multiregion. Thus, using the $n \equiv 16$ example values from above, G{0} is a 16x16 dense array, G{1} is an 8x8 strided-by-[2,2] array, etc. All levels have the index value (0,0) defined, though of course, level 5 has only this index position defined. See figure 7.2.

When multiarrays are used in expressions they must always have indices specified, though the index can be a general expression that evaluates to a nonnegative integer. Returning to an earlier example where elements of a dense array were aggregated into a

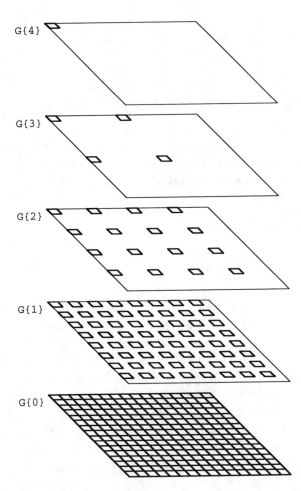

Figure 7.2
Visualization of hierarchical array G

strided-by-[2, 2] array, it is now possible to perform the same operation across successive levels of a single hierarchical array variable by using a loop,

```
for i = 1 to log2(n) do
   [H{i}]   G{i} := 0.4*G{i-1} + 0.25*G{i-1}@epow2{i-1}
              + 0.25*G{i-1}@spow2{i-1} + 0.1*G{i-1}@sepow2{i-1};
end;
```

assuming earlier declarations and the obvious definitions for the directions. As the loop proceeds, the strides of the region become longer and longer as the index references higher levels. The corresponding levels of the variable are referenced using an index in braces: On the left hand side the level's stride matches that of the region, while the levels referenced on the right-hand side are one level lower, i.e., shorter strides. The directions are indexed accordingly.

Permutations, Gather and Scatter

ZPL is designed so that the operations it provides are efficiently executed in parallel, and this fact has greatly influenced the form and type of its features. But, there are some inherently expensive computations that are nevertheless useful for solving problems, and they must be provided, too. Permutation—the ability to rearrange data—is an important example. In this section the permutation operator is explained. Programmers should use this operation whenever necessary, i.e., when no other way to achieve the same effect is obvious, but a warning is in order. *Permutation is the most expensive operator in ZPL.*

Consider the 1D array $I \equiv 6\ 5\ 4\ 3\ 2\ 1$ and the two 1D arrays V and W. If ZPL allowed array subscripts, then $V := W[I]$ might be expected to have the effect of selecting the items of W in reverse order, and assigning them to V; symmetrically $V[I] := W$ might be expected to assign the elements of W to V from last subscript to first, i.e., reversed. Thus, in both cases the contents of W are permuted into reverse order in V. In fact, these two operations can be expressed in ZPL using the gather and scatter forms of permutation

```
[1..6]   V := <##[I]W;
                 -- Gather W's items in reverse order, assign
[1..6]   V := >##[I]W;
                 -- Scatter W's items into V in reverse order
```

where ## is the permutation operator, I is the *reordering specifier* describing how the data is to be rearranged, and gather (<) and scatter (>) specify how the rearrangement is to be interpreted.

Consider another example, one in which gather and scatter have different effects.* Suppose `I ≡ 1 3 5 2 4 6` is an integer array, and `W` is the 6 element character array `a b c d e f`. Then

```
[1..6]    V := <##[I]W;   -- Gather - odd letters before evens
```

produces `a c e b d f` for `V`, since the `W` values will be gathered in this order and assigned, while

```
[1..6]    V := >##[I]W;
                         -- Scatter - interleave 1st 1/2, last 1/2
```

produces `a d b e c f` for `V`, since the values of `W` are scattered into the indicated index positions.

The permutation operator requires that the values of the permutation specifier `I` be defined indices for `W` in the case of gather, or defined indices of `V` in the case of scatter. Notice that `I` must be an integer array.

Arrays of higher dimension can be permuted by extending the concept of the reordering specifier to a sequence of arrays, one for the subscripts of each dimension. Thus, to permute the elements of a two dimensional array, two rectangular arrays would be provided giving the first and second elements of the subscripts. For example, let

```
           1 2 3 4                   1 1 1 1
Sub1 =     1 2 3 4      Sub2  =      2 2 2 2
           1 2 3 4                   3 3 3 3
           1 2 3 4                   4 4 4 4
```

be arrays, and `A` be a 4 × 4 array. Then

```
A := <##[Sub1, Sub2] A;
```

transposes `A`, since `Sub1` provides the first element of the index pairs and `Sub2` provides the second element. Thus, the `(4,3)` position of the result will be found in position `(3,4)` because the `(4,3)` element of `Sub1` is 3 and `(4,3)` element of `Sub2` is 4. The preferred way of expressing the transpose, as explained below, is to use the proper `Index`*d* values, as in

```
A := <##[Index2, Index1] A;        -- Transpose A
```

---

* Gather and scatter have the same effect when the permutation is an exchange, i.e., when the element in position *i* goes to position *j* and the element in *j* goes to *i*.

This not only saves the programmer the effort of constructing the two reordering arrays, but it is evident to the reader of the program that transposition is being performed, i.e., the indices are being reversed.

Generally, the elements of a d-dimensional array can be permuted by providing the order in which they should be gathered or the order in which they should be scattered as a d length sequence of d-dimensional arrays,

```
[A1, A2, ..., Ad]
```

such that the source (gather) or destination (scatter) of element

```
(i1, i2, ..., id)
```

is given by the index

```
(A1(i1,i2,...,id), A2(i1,i2,...,id), ..., Ad(i1,i2,...,id)).
```

That is, the jth array gives the index values for the jth dimension.

An important difference between gather and scatter is that the reordering indices of gather can contain repetitions, while the reordering indices of scatter should be distinct. Thus, given

```
[1..6]  I := 1;
```

the gather statement

```
[1..6]  V := <##[I] W; -- Set all of V to first element of W
```

is an expensive way to assign the first element of W to the elements of V, i.e., the value for each position is selected from the first position of W. (Flooding would have been preferred.) However, the scatter

```
[1..6]  V := >##[I]W;   -- UNPREDICTABLE scatter
```

is ill-defined. The statement asserts that the first item of V is to come from positions 1 through 6 of W, but since the order of array assignment is unspecified, it is unpredictable which value will actually be assigned. Though there is no check for uniqueness in the reordering specifier of scatters, nonunique reordering specifications should be avoided to assure deterministic computation.

As previously noted, when transposing an array, it is recommended that the reordering specifier be given by Indexd, as in

```
Atransp := <##[Index2, Index1]A;        -- Form A^T
```

Guidelines for More Efficient Use of Permutations

(a) *Constant reordering specifiers:* Reordering specifiers constructed from expressions involving constant operands, e.g., Index$d$, are preferred, as in

```
[1..n]  Bkwds := <##[n - Index1 + 1]Fwds; -- Reverse elements
```

(b) *Empty entries for subarrays:* If whole subarrays are to be reordered as a unit, e.g., reordering columns, leave the "identity" dimensions blank, as in

```
A := <##[ ,n-Index2+1] A;  -- Prefer'd to <##[Index1,n-Index2+1]A
```

which reorders the columns last-to-first.

(c) *Using Flood Arrays:* When whole subarrays are to be reordered as a unit, e.g., reordering columns, and the reordering specification cannot be given with a constant expression, use a flood array, as in

```
[*,1..n]  Fl := +<<[R] Counts;   -- Add entries to rank items
          A  := <##[ ,Fl] A;     -- Reorder A with ranks
```

since this can reduce set-up.

(d) *Repeated permutations:* If the same permutation is to be used multiple times, it is recommended that the reordering specifier arrays be set up together prior to executing any of the permutations and left unmodified.

Figure 7.3
Guidelines for permutations

The use of the Indexd arrays is not only clearer, it is also more efficient (than the user-created identifiers Sub1 and Sub2 from above), because the compiler can optimize the cost of setting up the permutation. Indeed, to the extent that programmers can realize their intended permutations in accordance with the suggestions in figure 7.3, the compiler will be aided in the set-up or the reordering.

8 WYSIWYG Parallel Execution

ZPL programmers write no parallel commands. When the program is executed on a parallel computer, the concurrency comes from the fact that the array operations can be performed in any order, including in parallel. The compiler arranges for the parallelism. This means that ZPL is an implicitly parallel language. It is possible to program ZPL without considering how the program will execute in parallel. But, it is advisable to consider parallel ZPL execution, because the characteristics that are preferred for parallel execution also promote high performance on modern sequential computers as well (caches, multi-issue instruction execution).

The previous chapters have concentrated on explaining the basics of ZPL's syntax and semantics. This chapter completes the picture. It is essential to have some idea of how a program will be executed, since presumably one wishes to select the most efficient way to realize the computation. Since ZPL is a machine independent language, it is not possible to describe program execution in seconds. Machines differ in clock rates, instructions set characteristics, etc. However, because ZPL's design is based on a hypothetical computer that resembles commercial parallel machines, it is possible to describe program execution in broad terms that are accurate enough to make effective programming decisions. The result is a better performing program. This chapter discusses ZPL program execution with respect to this idealization.

ZPL's property allowing programmers to know approximately how well their machine independent parallel program will perform has been dubbed "ZPL's what you see is what you get (WYSIWYG) performance model." This is perhaps one of the language's most powerful features. It is not available with any other parallel programming language.

Parallel Machine Model

Though ZPL was designed to be a machine independent parallel programming language, the design decisions were based on the assumption that the programs would be executed on an idealized parallel computer, the CTA, see figure 8.1. The CTA was developed to describe the fundamental properties of real parallel computers while ignoring irrelevant detail. The best way to decide how a ZPL program will perform, therefore, is to imagine that it is being executed by the CTA. By basing decisions on this abstract model, the same one used by the compiler writers, the programmer will be making the same assumptions that are used in the compiler. Since the compiler makes each real computer realize the properties of the CTA, the observed performance should approximate the assumed performance, to the greatest extent possible.

The CTA* machine is composed of P processors, each of which can be thought of as a standard sequential computer with the ability to execute instructions from its local

---

* CTA is mnemonic for the curious phrase, Candidate Type Architecture [Snyder 86].

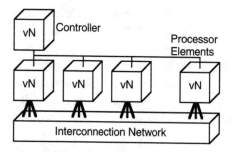

Figure 8.1
The CTA idealized parallel machine

memory. Thus, to understand how ZPL executes on a sequential computer, assume $P=1$ in the following.

The processors are connected together by an interconnection network. (This is assumed not to exist when $P=1$.) Though marketing literature often focuses on the topology and routing properties of a commercial computer's communication network, these details are not the concern of the ZPL programmer. So, they are left unspecified in the CTA machine model. Rather, the model states that a processor can reference its local memory in unit time, but references to the memory of another processor—whether by message passing or shared memory—requires λ time units, $\lambda \gg 1$. The value of λ is different for each machine, but typical values are two or more orders of magnitude more than a local (cache hit) memory reference, and sometimes as high as 4 orders of magnitude. ZPL's treatment of this performance difference between local and nonlocal memory references is discussed below.

In addition to the processor the CTA has a *controller.* This sequential machine, which has its own local memory, is attached to all processors, and could assist in certain global operations, such as reduce, scan, broadcast, etc. It can also serve as a repository for global data.

The CTA does not correspond to any physical computer, though some commercial computers are very similar. However, the capabilities of the CTA can be implemented efficiently on existing parallel computers, whether they be "shared memory" or "message passing" computers. Thus, if a programmer writes a ZPL program that would be efficient in concept on the CTA, the ZPL compiler should be able to generate object code for any real machine that is also efficient [Snyder 94].

For a ZPL program to run on a particular physical computer the compiler must be retargeted to that machine. (This is *not* a task performed by the ZPL programmer.) Retargeting mostly entails interfacing to existing vendor-produced software on the target parallel computer. The base compiler translates a ZPL program into ANSI C, which, using the retargeted libraries, etc., can be compiled by the native C compiler for the parallel machine. Given that the compiler has been retargeted, recompilation of the ZPL compiler's output is all that is required for a program to run on a new computer. In this way ZPL programs are completely portable.

Parallel Execution of ZPL

For the ZPL compiler to produce object code for a parallel computer, it must allocate data to the computer's memory. The main concern is how to allocate arrays. These are partitioned into sections that are allocated one section to each processor memory.

Memory Allocation

Scalars in ZPL are replicated across all processors, as are indexed arrays (see next section).

Parallel arrays in ZPL are partitioned by default into blocks. This partitioning is generally efficient for the operations available in ZPL. The exact blocked partitioning of the default allocation depends on the dimensionality of the array:

1-dimensional arrays: The index range including border regions is divided into P dense subsequences, allocated one per processor.

2-dimensional arrays: The array, including adjacent border regions, is divided into P dense 2-dimensional subarrays.

$k \geq 3$-dimensional arrays: Dimensions 1–k-2 are projected to 2 dimensions and allocated as 2-dimensional arrays.

Figure 8.2 illustrates these partitioning rules.

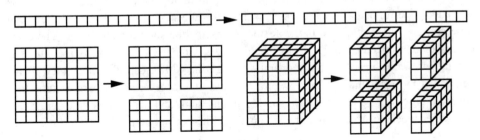

Figure 8.2
Partitioning of 1D, 2D and 3D arrays for allocation to memories of 4 processors

The first thing to notice is that because *P* is usually smaller than the size of interesting arrays, each processor will usually have multiple values stored in its memory, and these values will cover a dense set of indices. Further, values with the same index will be stored on the same processor. This allows typical ZPL computations, such as X := Y + Z, to be compiled so a processor can perform the computation by referencing only local data, i.e., without communicating with any other processor. For operations such as A@d, the compiler will usually have to produce data movement commands to transfer portions of the array across block boundaries, i.e., move data from processor to processor. However, because the partitioning has the form of dense blocks, most values will not have to move off of the processor. Further, the interprocessor transfer will move several values at once, which is usually more efficient than moving a single value at a time [Choi & Snyder 97].

Processor Code

In *concept* the ZPL program can be thought of as executing on the controller processor of the CTA. In this view the scalar variables are stored in the controller's memory, and the (parallel) arrays are stored in the memories of the other processors. The controller stages the execution of the statements. The processors perform those portions of each statement that apply to data that is stored on that processor. This view is only conceptual to aid in organizing the computation.

In actuality ZPL uses a single program, multiple data (SPMD) form of parallelism, i.e., the compiler generates a single program that is replicated on each processor.* Expressions involving only scalars or indexed arrays are executed by each processor. The compiler creates code for expressions involving regions so that each processor performs that portion of the computation applicable to index values of data stored in its memory. When @, wrap, reflect, flood, reduce, scan or permutation operations are required, data transfer instructions are usually performed [Chamberlain et al. 1996].

The reduce and scan operations are performed in multiple steps. In the first step, the operation is performed on local data. Thus, in +<<A the sum of the values stored on each processor is computed locally. In the next step these partial sums are combined. The exact details of this operation differ from machine to machine: On some machines there is special hardware to perform these operations, e.g., the CM-5. On other machines, this is performed by a combining "tree" where a group of processors send partial sums to a common processor which produces another partial sum, and passes this new sum along to another processor to continue the summation. This technique produces the final result

---

* SMPD differs from SIMD in that the processors need not execute the same instruction simultaneously, but rather describe their own path of execution through the common program.

in one processor. In the last step of reduce, the result is broadcast back so that it is known to the other processors. The scan is analogous, though somewhat more complex.

Estimating Program Performance

As with most computer programs it is not possible to know *exactly* how fast a ZPL program will run without executing it on the actual machine, and the performance will vary from machine to machine. But it is possible to make a rough performance estimate based on which operations are expensive and inexpensive. Here, we present the basic performance properties of ZPL.

Full Concurrency

Like most languages, the execution time for array operations is proportional to the number of scalar instructions required to implement the array operation. Thus, the basic computation of the Cannon's algorithm matrix multiplication program from figure 6.3

```
[Res]    C := C + A*B;
```

will require approximately *mn* multiply instructions, *mn* add instructions together with roughly *3mn* loads and *mn* stores to move the operand values from the memory back and forth to the processor. There is also a small amount of overhead required to implement the implied looping.

If the operations are performed on a parallel computer and are roughly evenly divided among P processors according to the partitioning described in the last section, then the programmer can expect about P-way speed up. That is, the computation will achieve essentially full concurrency. The two properties that ensure this desirable result for this statement are

Only element-wise array operations are used, and
All operands refer to elements of the same region.

Statements with these properties should exhibit excellent performance. As a further assessment for such statements, the performance on a sequential computer is approximately the same as it would be if the equivalent C program had been written.

Notice that when the arrays are flood arrays the situation can actually be slightly better than described above. Specifically, in the SUMMA algorithm matrix computation, statement 13 of figure 6.5

```
[M]    C := C + Af*Bf;
```

would normally be expected to have the same cost as the analogous Cannon's algorithm statement from above. But because the flood arrays, Af and Bf, are represented by their defining values, the repeated references to these values will "hit" in the cache, giving excellent cache behavior.

"@" References

The "@" operator when applied to an operand generally causes some data values to be communicated between processors. The key property of this nearest neighbor communication is that typically only a few values are transmitted per processor. For example, when the local portion of array A allocated to processor P_i is a 10×10 block, the execution of the statement A := A@east requires that 10 values be received from the eastern neighbor and 10 values be sent to the western neighbor assuming the 2D allocation of figure 8.2. Though the whole array is logically shifted, only a fraction of the values are required to change processors and incur communication costs. The schematic in figure 8.3 illustrates that only the items along the "edge" of a local block allocation need to be sent for a "shift by 1." The actual amount of data sent for any @ reference depends on the array's size, allocation and the direction. Moreover, it often happens that a given @ reference will not induce any communication because a previous reference has already caused the communication to be performed, and the compiler recognizes that the values are still cached [Choi & Snyder 97].

Thus, the nearest neighbor communication generally entails transmitting only "surface" items of the local allocation, and so performs best on those allocations where the surface-to-volume ratio is most favorable. Though more expensive than statements not involving communication, statements involving "@" operators are efficiently implemented and relatively inexpensive [Chamberlain, Choi & Snyder 97].

Note that from the point of view of estimating execution time, the wrap and reflect operations should also be considered to be nearest neighbor operations.

Strided Regions

In general, operations over strided regions perform as well as the analogous operations over non-strided regions, except they are sparser. That is, because a strided array has fewer elements than a dense array, e.g., a 2D array strided by two in each dimension has one-quarter as many elements as the dense array of the same index ranges, there is proportionately less work performed. Strided arrays are allocated "by index," which means that element (i, j) of Astride is stored on the same processor as element (i, j) of Adense. Thus, strided arrays are naturally load-balanced. Strided arrays are stored densely, and so exhibit locality beneficial to caching.

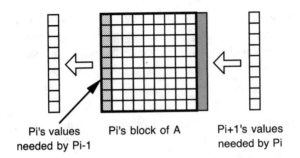

Pi's values   Pi's block of A   Pi+1's values
needed by Pi-1   needed by Pi

Figure 8.3
Schematic diagram of the values transferred to processor P_i from P_{i+1} and from P_i to P_{i-1} in evaluating
`A := A@east`

Reductions/Scans

The algorithms implementing reduce and scan begin by performing the operation on the block of local data as an intermediate computation. For example, the operation `+<<A` causes each processor to add up the local elements of A allocated to it. The result(s) of the local computations are then globally combined. The details of how this is done vary widely depending on the characteristics of the available hardware. In any case the combining will usually use a technique called the parallel prefix algorithm. This produces a single, global result that is then broadcast back to each processor. In the case of reduction the computation is complete, but for a scan the local values must be updated using the returned intermediate values.

The local portion of the computation will run about as fast as the expression, `c+A`. The global portion, though difficult to estimate, will generally involve an "accumulation tree," and a "broadcast tree" composed of processors. These trees tend to limit concurrency, since generally only processors at a given "level" in the accumulation tree can be active simultaneously. Thus, reduce and scan are more expensive operations than @ references. Of course, they are also among the most powerful operations in the language, and generally worth their cost.

When executed sequentially, reduce and scan are implemented in a direct and efficient manner. As observed in the context of the computation in chapter 4, on parallel machines it can be that reduce and scan are more effective than repeated computations involving cheaper operations.

Flooding

As mentioned frequently, flood arrays are represented using only the defining values, i.e., by storing the lower dimensional arrays. So, for example, when a row is replicated by flooding, only the values of that row are stored in the flood array. If necessary, these values will be broadcast to other processors. Though some computers have special assistance for this operation, generally it should be seen as somewhat more expensive than using an "@" operation, but less expensive than performing a reduction or scan.

Scalar computations

Scalar quantities are replicated on each processor. Statements involving only scalar values, such as

```
i := i+1;
theta := pi/4;
```

are repeated on each processor. There is no parallelism with this approach, but it is not really feasible to achieve any anyway. Notice that the advantage of replicating the computation compared to computing it on one processor and broadcasting the value is that the replicated computation requires no communication.

Indexed arrays are replicated on each processor like scalars. This makes indexed arrays very efficient for representing tables and other constant data used in computations, because one copy is cached per processor, eliminating the need to communicate the values. See the use of the code book, CB, in the vector quantization data compression computation of chapter 6.

Since ZPL without parallel arrays is mostly a routine sequential language, it is clear that it is perfectly adequate for writing programs for sequential computers. In fact, if the program is not to be run on a parallel computer, then it can be written entirely using indexed arrays and the usual looping. The resulting program's performance will be about the same as a C program for the sequential machine. There is no parallelism, but this suggests a development approach: write a program using whatever mixture of parallel and indexed arrays that the programmer finds convenient subject to the goal of maximizing the use of parallel arrays. This program will run well on sequential machines. Then, the uses of indexed arrays can be converted to parallel arrays later when a parallel machine is to be used.

Permutations

The gather and scatter operations (##) are the most expensive operations in ZPL, because they can potentially generate two phases of all-to-all communication. They are nevertheless useful, and it is often the case that there is no efficient alternative to their use. For example, it is possible to write a transpose without using the permutation operator, but the communication required for transposition is inherently expensive on virtually all computers. So, permutation is as efficient as any solution.

I/O

Input and output are expensive in ZPL, just as in all other programming languages. One feature of I/O is that it is one of the few places where the ZPL compiler generates a barrier synchronization.

Summary on Estimation

Though it is not possible to precisely compute *a priori* the performance of a machine independent program, estimation is possible. For example, the two matrix multiplication programs given in the last chapter can be compared based on the guidelines presented here. Note that for the basic computation, both Cannon's algorithm and the SUMMA algorithm are about the same time, with some slight advantage to SUMMA for computing with a flood array. This is partly negated by the slightly greater time to flood as compared with shifting the array. So, the two algorithms are essentially the same time at their cores. However, the Cannon algorithm requires that the two arrays first be restructured into a staggered form. This operation is not necessary in the SUMMA code. So, even though this is only a moderately expensive operation, it is clear that the SUMMA algorithm will be more efficient [Chamberlain et al., 1998].

Closing Remarks on Performance

Because of basic properties of the ZPL language design, the compiler is capable of producing efficient code. Further, it can perform a variety of optimizations to reduce both the memory requirements and execution time of the object program. However, *nothing contributes to high performance like a thoughtfully written program*. Thus, the programmer is the most effective optimizer.

The CTA machine model, the brief descriptions of memory allocation, program organization and communication given earlier in this chapter describe approximately how the ZPL compiler is likely to organize an object program. It is advisable to keep the following additional points in mind when making performance decisions during programming.

· Maximize the use of (parallel) arrays and array-based computation.

· Use reduce and scan moderately, since they limit concurrency.

· Use permute sparingly.

· Express the program directly and succinctly, resisting the temptation to "program for your implementation."

The last point cannot be emphasized too much. Most optimizations rely on the compiler being successful at analyzing a segment of the program. Programs that are convoluted or that use structures designed to "trick" a particular compiler into producing specific results will almost certainly frustrate the analysis of other compilers and greatly limit the program's portability. If the program is as clean as a classroom example, the compiler is likely to produce textbook example optimizations.

References

B. Chamberlain, S. Choi, E Lewis, C. Lin, L. Snyder and W.Weathersby, 1996, "Factor-Join: A Unique Approach to Compiling Array Languages for Parallel Machines." *Proceedings of Languages and Compilers for Parallel Computers,* Springer-Verlag.

Bradford L. Chamberlain, Sung-Eun Choi, E Christopher Lewis, Calvin Lin, Lawrence Snyder and W. Derrick Weathersby, 1998, "ZPL's WYSIWYG Performance Model," *Proceedings of the IEEE Workshop on High-Level Parallel Programming Models and Supportive Environments (HIPS'98).*

B. Chamberlain, S. Choi and L. Snyder, 1997, "IRONMAN: An Architecture Independent Communication Interface for Parallel Computers," Workshop on Languages and Compilers for Parallel Computers, Springer-Verlag.

Sung-Eun Choi and Lawrence Snyder, 1997, "Quantifying the Effects of Communication Optimizations," *International Conference on Parallel Processing.*

L. Snyder, 1986, "Type Architecture, Shared Memory and the Corollary of Modest Potential," *Annual Review of Computer Science,* vol. I, Annual Reviews Inc., pp. 289–318.

L. Snyder, 1994, "Foundations of Practical Parallel Programming Languages," In J. Ferrante and A. J. G. Hey (eds.), *Portability and Performance for Parallel Processing,* John Wiley & Sons, Ltd., pp. 1–19.

9 Computational Techniques

As has been observed previously, ZPL is an expressive language that simplifies programming because it saves the programmer from specifying many low level details like looping and indexing. Perhaps more importantly, by leaving these low level details unspecified, the programmer allows the compiler the freedom to organize the object code to take advantage of the target computer's features. The result is good performance and complete machine independence. So, there is a strong incentive to become fluent in ZPL's high level programming style.

In the interest of presenting more examples of high level programming style, this chapter presents a series to "typical programming situations" and their solutions in ZPL. The computations considered are

Sequential Computation
Inconsequential Code Fragments
Sequential routines for promotion

N-Body Computations

Thinking Globally—Median Finding

Random Number Generation

Programming situations in one area of scientific programming may never arise in another, so the topics may not apply to all programmers. Nevertheless, they are sufficiently generic, that studying each closely will generally provide concepts and knowledge that can be applied often.

Sequential Computation

Achieving parallelism in scientific computations is sufficiently difficult that this guide has missed few opportunities to comment on the parallel implications of a ZPL concept or construct. But, not every program must run on a parallel supercomputer, nor does every part of a supercomputer computation have to run in parallel. In such situations, ZPL is a fine sequential programming language, too.

"Sequential" program text in ZPL is code that will not run in parallel. As a general rule computations not involving (parallel) arrays will be sequential. Computations employing only scalars and/or indexed arrays are the primary instances of sequential text. For example,

```
area := pi * (diam / 2) ^ 2;      -- All variables are scalar
```

and

```
for i := 1 to m do            -- SEQUENTIAL matrix multiply
  for j := 1 to p do          -- using indexed arrays
    for k := 1 to n do        --
      C[i,j] := C[i,j] + A[i,k]*B[k,j];
```

are sequential ZPL text. This is evident since the computations do not use (parallel) arrays.

Sequential and parallel computations, though compiled differently, will perform about the same on a single processor computer. On a parallel computer, sequential computations are replicated. That is, each processor performs the sequential computations redundantly. Thus, sequential and parallel code can be freely intermixed, and when it is executed on parallel computers, there will be no overhead for the sequential computations, nor (unfortunately) any speed-up.

Two common cases arise where ZPL programmers find themselves writing significant amounts of sequential code: inconsequential code fragments, and sequential routines for promotion. Each will be illustrated.

Inconsequential Code Fragments

There are components of a computation that do not represent a significant fraction of the overall work, but are nevertheless essential to a fully operational program. Examples include initialization and problem set up, assessing termination or continuation conditions at the end of loops, error correction or recovery, etc. It is not essential that there be a fully parallel solution for these components because they contribute so little to the overall running time. Indeed, for many of these computations, there probably does not exist a parallel solution, and even if there does, it may take more time to launch it than can be recovered through speedup. These computations can and should be performed sequentially.

As an example, consider an array A whose m rows must be rearranged before the start of the computation, so that the 0th column is in ascending order. This might represent a situation where the 0th column gives key properties about where the data was collected, e.g., latitude.

Since it is assumed that the number m of rows, (but perhaps not their length n) is a smallish number, it is decided to perform the sort sequentially. (There are parallel sorts, but m is small enough that it is presumed that doing so is not advantageous.) The solution is to assign the 0th column values into the indexed array Order[1..m], sort them sequentially, flood the order into a parallel array and then permute the array.

The indexed array Order is declared

```
var     Order : array [1..m] of pairs;
        temp  : pairs;
```

where `pairs` is declared

```
type pairs = record
   val : float;
   tag : integer;
end;
```

to have a `val` field and a `tag` field. The value will contain the 0th column information. The tag is to be initialized to an integer giving the initial order of the data, and hence the rows. The values and tags are sequentially initialized,

```
for i := 1 to m do
  [i,0] Order[i].val := +<< A;      -- Val selected from col 0
        Order[i].tag := i;          -- Tag gives initial order
  end;
```

Notice that the contents of the 0th column of the parallel array are extracted and assigned to the sequential array's fields using reduction over a singleton region. The reduce may seem peculiar, but it is (purposely) the only way to assign a parallel array value to a sequential variable, as a reminder that a broadcast to all processors is required. (See chapter 8.)

With `Order` initialized, it is sorted sequentially

```
for i := 1 to m-1 do               -- Sort
  for j := 2 to m do               --    using a
    if Order[i].val > Order[j].val  --    standard
      then                         --    exchange
          temp     := Order[i];    --    sort
          Order[i] := Order[j];    --    which is
          Order[j] := temp;        --    sequential
      end;                         --    since
    end;                           --    Order is an
end;                               --    indexed array
```

Any sequential sort will suffice.

At this point the `val` fields are in sequence, and the tag field of item i tells which original row of A is to become row i in the reordered A. To implement this reordering, the tags are stored in a flood array

```
[1..m,*]  Perm := Order[Index1].tag;   -- Load order from
                                        -- indexed to parallel array
```

in preparation for reordering. Notice that the indexed array is subscripted by a parallel array, yielding a parallel result. There is no communication for this statement since each processor has a copy of `Order`. The rows are then permuted using the gather form of permutation

```
[1..m,0..n] A := <## [Perm, ] A;       -- Reorder rows
```

The second reordering array is elided, indicating that the entire row is be moved as a unit. These last two statements are parallel computations, which could be combined

```
[1..m,0..n]  A := <## [Order[Index1].tag, ] A;
                                        -- Reorder rows
```

saving the creation of the `Perm` variable.

Sequential Routines for Promotion

A common way to realize a parallel computation is by performing many instances of a basic sequential computation on the elements of a parallel array. In such cases the base computation will use the sequential components of ZPL. These are then applied to the elements of a parallel array by promotion to achieve the parallel result. This idea has been applied before in the distance computation for Vector Quantization of chapter 6. It is sufficiently important, however, that it deserves another example.

This illustration will use an optimal global substring match, which is a representative computation from the genome sequencing applications area. The task is to locate the best match of a length m candidate sequence *Can* in a length n primary sequence *Prime*, $m \ll n$. In concept the problem can be solved by considering how well *Can* matches the first m letters of *Prime*, i.e., $Prime_{1..m}$ and giving it a score, and considering how well *Can* matches $Prime_{2..m+1}$ and $Prime_{3..m+2}$, etc. throughout the whole primary sequence, and then selecting the position with the highest score.

Can: CAT
Prime: GGCACACTTTCAGTCAAGATATGGTAGACCCACC
         └── Match against candidate sequence

Obviously, the subroutine for this computation is to figure the score of the *Can* string against a substring of the *Prime* string.

Figure 9.1
Matches of CAT against GCAT starting at the first and second positions

This "match" operation is actually a little more complicated than determining if two letter sequences are identical. Rather, insertions and deletions of letters are allowed, so two strings are scored by their degree of similarity. For example, the candidate string CAT matches the primary string GCAT beginning at the first position by assuming either that there was an insertion of G in the primary sequence or the deletion of a G in the candidate sequence. The candidate matches exactly when beginning at the second letter of the primary sequence, of course. Since this latter is a more direct match than the former, it is scored higher. Approximate matching, therefore, can be applied to strings of different length.

The conceptual process behind computing the approximate match between two strings S and T is to imagine filling out a table, in which position i,j gives the score for $S[1..i]$ compared against $T[1..j]$. An indexed array, V, serves as the table with a row for each S letter and a column for each T letter. (A 0th position handles the case of zero letters, denoted by ε.) See figure 9.1.

After initializing the corner element to zero, a table entry is computed from the preceding entries by crediting +2 for a match or −1 for a mismatch. Thus, a table entry i,j is the maximum (best guess) of three quantities:

$$V[i,j] = \max \begin{cases} V[i-1,j]-1 & \text{Assumes insertion in S or deletion in T} \\ \text{if } S[i]=T[j] \text{ then } V[i-1,j-1]+2 \text{ else } V[i-1,j-1]-1 \\ V[i,j-1]-1 & \text{Assumes deletion in S, or insertion in T} \end{cases}$$

Both of the insertion/deletion cases are instances of mismatches. The initial values for the 0th row and the 0th column are simply the scores assuming deletions in S and T (respectively) up to the given position. The result is the lower right corner table entry, i.e., $V[m,n]$.

A key observation is that the whole table does not have to be kept, since by filling it out column-wise, only the previous column or the previous entry in the same column is ever referenced. Hence, only one column needs to be represented, motivating the sequential procedure shown in figure 9.2 to compute the score.

```
 1 procedure score(
 2             var S : array[0..m] of ubyte,-- Indexed array of string
 3               pos : shortint,            -- Position of T considered
 4             var t : ubyte,               -- Letter in T[pos]
 5             var V : array [0..m] of shortint --Index array of col
below
 6                                          -- T[pos-1] updated to T[pos]
 7                   ) : shortint;          -- Return the best score
 8     var  i,                              -- Index
 9         best,                            -- Highest score in column
10         mtch,                            -- Temp to compute match
11         last: shortint;                  -- Temp to save previous
entry
12 begin
13     last  := V[0];                       --    from overwrite
14     V[0]  := - pos;                      -- Initialize first entry
15     best  := - pos;                      -- Initialize maximum score
16     for i := 1 to m do                   -- Working down the column
17         if S[i] = t then mtch := 2 else mtch := -1 end;
18         mtch := mtch + last;             -- Result of compare + diag
19         last := V[i];                    -- Grab next before overwrite
20         V[i]:=max3(mtch,V[i-1]-1,V[i]-1);-- Compute scores, pick max
21         if V[i] > best then best := V[i] end;-- Save best score
22     end;
23     return best;                         -- Report back
24 end;


 1 procedure max3(x, y, z : shortint) : shortint;
 2 begin
 3  if x >= y & x >= z then return x; end;
 4  if y >= x & y >= z then return y; end;
 5  if z >= x & z >= y then return z; end;
 6 end;
```

Figure 9.2
The score procedure and the auxiliary max3 procedure

This sequential procedure score takes the S string and one letter of the T string as "by-reference" (var) parameters, meaning they will be referenced externally and not actually "passed in." Additionally, the position, pos, of the letter t from the start of string T is passed in for use in initializing the 0th entry in the column. The column V is also referenced externally. The logic of the routine is simply to work down the column, using the previous entries to create new ones.

To put the whole computation together, the sequential procedure score will be applied at each position of the primary string, producing a parallel computation. First, data structures for the candidate and primary strings are declared

```
var   Can : [0..m] array of ubyte;
                            -- Indexed array for Candidate
     Prime : [1..n] ubyte;       -- Parallel array for Primary
      Vee : [1..n] array [0..m] of shortint;
```

```
                              -- Parallel array of indexed
                              -- arrays representing a
                              -- column of each table
    Best : [1..n] shortint;   -- Parallel array of scores
```

as well as the parallel array `Vee` of columns. The ith element of `Vee` will represent the current (`pos`) column of the table for the match starting at the ith position of `Prime`, its maximum score to this point will be in the ith element of `Best`. After declaring a

```
direction right = [1];
```

and initializing `Best` and all of the columns of `Vee` to their proper 0th column values,

```
Best   := 0;
for i := 0 to m do Vee[i] := -i; end;
```

the data can be read in. Once `Can` and `Prime` contain their proper letter strings, the loop

```
for j := 1 to m do
[1..n-j+1]  Best  := max(Best, score(Can, j, Prime, Vee));
  [1..n-j]  Prime := Prime@right;
  end;
```

produces the desired result. (The iteration would likely continue beyond `m` cycles to provide for insertions in T.)

The `score` procedure is called with parallel arrays `Prime` and `Vee` corresponding to scalar `t` and indexed array `V`, respectively, in the procedure header. This creates a parallel computation in which the sequential procedure is promoted to apply to each position. The use of "by-reference" parameters assures that there will be but one copy of the basic data structures. The shift of `Prime` brings the next letter position into consideration. Notice that the regions limit the computation to those positions of `Prime` for which the `Can` string does not "fall off of the end."

The relevant entries for `Vee` assuming `Can` ≡ CAT and `Prime` ≡ GCAT are

```
  0   0   0   0      -1 -1 -1 -1      -2  -2  -2  x      -3 -3  x  x
 -1  -1  -1  -1      -1  2 -1 -1       1   1   2  x       0  0  x  x
 -2  -2  -2  -2      -2  1 -2 -2       0   4   3  x       3  3  x  x
 -3  -3  -3  -3      -3  0 -3 -3      -1   3   4  x       2  6  x  x
      Initial            j=1              j=2                j=3
```

Notice that columns 1 and 2 in each snapshot correspond to the ith columns in the tables shown in figure 9.1.

Of course, the best score is found by

```
... max<< Best ...
```

and the positions of the best matches are given by the nonzero items in the expression

```
... Index1*(Best = max<<Best) ...
```

which could be printed out or participate in other computations.

In summary, ZPL keeps a reasonably strict separation between the parallel and sequential features of the language so that programmers can always be aware of how their code will be executed. However, by promoting sequential computations to apply to the elements of parallel arrays, efficient parallel computations are created.

N-Body Computations

Many problems involve the motion of bodies in space. If space can be uniformly decomposed, the most straightforward ZPL representation is an array whose elements are lists of the bodies. The array represents the decomposition of space, and the body lists are maintained in user-managed indexed arrays. Each cell in the decomposition is processed in parallel, making this an instance of the promoted sequential routines discussed in the last section. This N-body solution is most effective when certain properties are present:

· If every cell of the decomposition contains a reasonable number of bodies and the ratio between the number of bodies in the sparsest to densest cell is not too extreme, e.g., 1:3, say, rather than 1:10,000, then the work will be balanced.

· If there is a reliable (though perhaps not perfect) upper limit on the number of bodies in a block, then the storage allocated for the lists can be managed more easily.

Many, but not all N-body problems fulfill these conditions. Even when they do not, ZPL can be used for a solution, though the performance might fall below expectations.

To illustrate sample N-body computations, postulate that 2D space has been decomposed into an $n \times n$ mesh of cells, and that the maximum number of bodies in any cell is m. (The generalization to 3D is obvious.)

```
constant m: integer = 100;   -- max particles per cell
         n: integer = 16;    -- # of cells on side of mesh
```

These parameters are assigned typical values, which will probably be revised when tuning the program for performance. The region of the computation is

```
region R = [1..n, 1..n];     -- Problem mesh, representing
                             -- partitioned 2D space
```

The array containing the m-element lists of bodies

```
var     Parts: [R] array [1..m] of particle;
```

is declared, where a `particle` is represented by a record

```
type particle = record       -- Particles are triples of
             x,               -- Position x coord
             y,               -- Position y coord
             v: float end;    -- and value
```

containing three values. True N-body computations would use more complete representations for the bodies, of course, but these suffice here.

Each cell will, generally, not have exactly 100 particles in it, so it is necessary to keep a count of the number of particles actually present. This count is also a (parallel) array because there is a different count for each cell. Continuing the variable declarations,

```
C:   [R] shortint;      -- Particles per cell <= 16K
```

provides a short integer for the count for each cell, as illustrated in figure 9.3.

An important programming convention will be that the particles will be kept at the "front" of the lists, with the unused particle positions at the higher indices. Thus, elements of `Parts` that are occupied have index positions `1..C`.

The coordinates of each cell in space will be represented by the positions of its lower left and upper right corners. These could be represented by records with a pair of values for each corner's *x,y* coordinates, but since the coordinates are never used as a unit, bundling them together is unnecessary. Arrays of scalar values are, therefore, preferred.

```
LoX, LoY, HiX, HiY: [R]   float;
```

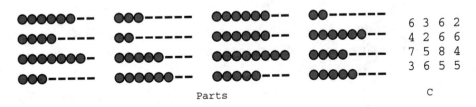

Parts   C

Figure 9.3
Illustration of `Parts` and `C` arrays for n = 4, m = 8

Though `shortint` might seem to be a better choice than float when space has been decomposed into integral sizes, it is more efficient to use `float` arrays to reduce type conversions in comparisons with elements of `Parts`.

To complete the declarations, array temporaries and a scalar index are defined.

```
Temp: [R] particle;
T, P: [R] shortint;
   i:     shortint;
```

`Temp` is an array that stores one particle per index position, `T` is another array storing an index of a particle list position, `P` is a flag array indicating (1 or 0) whether or not a moving particle has been found, and `i` is a scalar loop index.

Single Particle Pushing

To illustrate basic N-body manipulations, consider implementing the motion of single particles moving out of cells in a single direction, say `north`. This solution can be generalized to move more particles in multiple directions. The approach is to iterate (for all cells in parallel) through the particle lists looking for a particle whose updated position is outside the cell to the `north`. Those that are found, are removed from the lists, the lists are compacted to keep them dense, and the counts of particles are corrected. The particles are then sent to their neighbors and incorporated into the particle lists at the destinations. The computation has the following components:

· Initialization

· Find a departing particle

· Compact the list

· Move the particle

· Incorporate it into its new cell

These components will now be described. The overall one-direction, one-particle code is shown in figure 9.4.

Initialization. It is assumed the computation is underway, and that the positions of all particles have been updated. Those whose new position is beyond the limits of their cell are to be moved. The initialization is

```
T := C + 1;      -- Start position of mover 1 past end
P := 0;          -- Flag for found particle set at none
```

which indicate that no departing particle has yet been found.

```
 1  [R] begin                /* Initialize */
 2  T := C + 1;              -- Start position of mover 1 past end
 3  P := 0;                  -- Flag for found particle set at none
 4
 5         /* Find Departed Particle */
 6  for i := 1 to C do       -- Loop thru particles of each cell
 7    if Parts[i].y > HiY     -- Particle headed N?
 8      then                  -- Yes
 9        P := 1;             -- Record that one has been found
10        Temp := Parts[i];   -- Grab the particle
11        T := i;             -- Record where it is located
12        exit;               -- Interrupt loop as particle found
13    end;
14  end;
15
16         /* If Vacated, Compact list */
17  for i := T+1 to C do      -- Loop from point of interruption
18    Parts[i-1] := Parts[i]; --Scooch 'em up
19  end;
20  C := C - P;              -- Reduce count if particle left
21
22         /* Move Particle */
23  Temp := Temp@south;       -- Send particle N
24  P := P@south;             -- Send indicator of arrived point
25
26         /* Incorporate particle */
27  C := C + P;              -- If particle arrived, bump count
28  Parts[C+1-P] := Temp;     -- Add to list, or no-op if none
29  end;
```

Figure 9.4
One-particle-per-cell solution for pushing points north

Find departing particles.   Shattered control flow, indicated by the use of the array C in the for-loop statement, is used to sweep through the particle lists of the cells looking for a north moving particle.

```
        /* Find Departed Particle */
for i := 1 to C do       -- Loop thru particles of each cell
  if Parts[i].y > HiY     -- Particle headed north?
    then                  -- Yes
      P := 1;             -- Record that one has been found
      Temp := Parts[i];   -- Grab the particle
      T := i;             -- Record where it is located
      exit;               -- Interrupt loop as particle found
  end;
end;
```

Recall that since this is a shattered for-loop, there are n^2 (parallel) iterations, one for each cell, ranging over the intervals 1 to C, i.e., the loop for cell u,v ranges from 1 to $C_{u,v}$. The y coordinate of the ith particle in the list is compared with the HiY coordinate of the upper right corner of the cell. The loop is exited for each cell when a departing particle is discovered.

Compact the lists. It is presumed that some particles are departing, i.e., T != C+1, though it is not necessary. The vacated space is compacted, using another shattered for-loop.

```
            /* If Vacated, Compact list */
for i := T+1 to C do        -- Loop from point of interruption
   Parts[i-1] := Parts[i];  -- Scooch 'em up
end;
C := C - P;                 -- Reduce count if particle left
```

Having initialized T to be one position beyond the end of the list, i.e., C+1, the compaction loop falls through in the case no north moving particle was discovered in a give cell.

Move the particles. To move particles to the north requires that both their motion and the effects along the borders be considered. An assignment such as

```
Temp@north := Temp;      -- Send particle north
```

would seem to be the obvious statement, but it has the effect of modifying the north border of Temp plus all elements of the Temp array except the bottom row, i.e., it doesn't incorporate particles from the south border. Assuming that particles are to be lost when they move off the top edge, and that particles are to be introduced along the south edge

```
[R at south] Temp@north := Temp;   -- Send particles north
```

would have the proper affect provided the southern border of Temp had been set up to introduce particles. The right-hand side of the statement would refer to the southerly cells from which particles come, while the left-hand side would simply refer to Temp, i.e., the @north and at south cancel. An entirely equivalent construction, and probably somewhat more transparent, is

```
Temp:= Temp@south;       -- Get particles moving north
```

which focuses on where the particles are coming from rather than where they are going to. This is the desired construction, and we apply it a second time to record the arrival of a particle

```
P := P@south;       -- Indicate arriving particle
```

Notice that even when no particles are moving, the `Temp` array will transmit values. These are meaningless, which is why transmitting P, the indicator of useful data, is also required. It is possible to set up the computation to move actual particles only, but this is probably more expensive than treating them uniformly.

Incorporate new point. After the particles have been moved to the neighbor, the processing continues to include the newly arrived particle in the list.

```
                    /* Incorporate particle */
C := C + P;                    -- If particle arrived, bump count
Parts[C+1-P] := Temp;          -- Add to list, or no-op if none
```

P is 1 if a valid particle was sent, and 0 otherwise, so adding it to C changes the count only for those cells where points just arrived. By indexing `Parts` as shown, `Temp` is incorporated as the new last item (valid data sent and P=1), or unknown values are stored in the first free position of the particle list (invalid data sent and P=0).

The one-particle-per-cell solution is complete. It will sweep through the entire particle list for each cell removed. This is perhaps too much "work" for the result achieved. Removing more items at a time will reduce the overall computational work, and lead to a more efficient program.

Batched Pushing Solution

Generalizing the one-particle-per-cell solution is straightforward. The number of particles to be treated in a batch will be a parameter to the computation, so that the program can be conveniently customized to be optimal for the target computer. The declaration

```
constant b: integer = 5;       -- # of particles in batch
```

is to be added to the variable declarations section given above.

Next, the `Temp` variable, which is used to hold and transmit the particles, must be redeclared to have space enough to store the whole batch. The previous declaration for `Temp` is revised as follows

```
Temp: [R] array [1..b] of particle;
```

upgrading `Temp` to a (parallel) array of b-element linear arrays, each element being a particle.

Finally, by reinterpreting the flag array P from signaling that a moving particle has been found to counting the number of moving particles found, the previous code is easily rewritten. See figure 9.5. Indeed, notice that the one-particle-per-cell program can be interpreted as the batch size of 1 case, i.e., b = 1.

There are two noticeable changes to the program. First, as the particle list is scanned looking for moving particles, the loop is not interrupted until a full batch is formed. So, part of the compaction operation is incorporated into the search loop. The loop is exited when the batch has filled. The other change is in the code incorporating arrived particles into the list. The previous assignment became a loop, and it was more convenient to update the count variable after the items have been added. Notice that if no variables are sent, control falls through the loop and updating the count is a no-op.

The application of this program is as follows. The batch size b is set to, say, the expected number of north moving points, determined through some experimentation. Then, batches are moved in a loop which continues as long as north moving particles remain in any cell, i.e., 0 != +<<P. The concept is that for problems meeting the properties mentioned at the beginning, a small number of iterations (2–3) should suffice to move the particles. This doubtless leads to a more efficient solution that doing the transfer all at once, which would require a worst-case batch size, and is far more expedient than writing ZPL code to work out the actual number of items moving and then transferring the exact number. The principle is that in parallel computing it is often more effective to perform some redundant computation to reduce the critical path.

Thinking Globally—Median Finding

Finding the median of a set of numbers is a simple computation when the set has been sorted—select the middle item. But, if the set does not need to be sorted for other reasons, then the median can be found directly. The following program finds the median directly by keeping an interval lo:hi that bounds the median, estimating the median by the midpoint of the interval, computing which half contains the median and then collapsing the interval by "discarding" the other half. Convergence is achieved when the endpoints meet. Though this is a simple computation, it provides an opportunity to illustrate thinking globally.

The solution requires a linear region,

```
region R = [1..n];
```

the array containing the data and an array for masking,

```
var A : [R] float;
    M : [R] ubyte;
```

and some scalar variables to support the computation,

```
var lo,
    hi,
```

```
 1 [R] begin                   /* Initialize */
 2         T := C + 1;              -- Start interrupt position at end+1

 3         P := 0;                  -- Number found starts at 0

 4
 5                 /* Find Departed Particles */
 6     for i := 1 to C do          -- Loop thru particles of each cell
 7       if Parts[i].y > HiY       -- Particle headed N?
 8         then                    -- Yes
 9           P := P + 1;           -- Record that one has been found
10           Temp[P] := Parts[i];  -- Grab particle
11           T := i;               -- Record where it is located
12           if P=b then exit; end;-- Interrupt loop since batch filled

13         else
14           Parts[i-P] := Parts[i];      --Scooch up particles
15       end;
16     end;

17
18                 /* Complete Compacting list */
19     for i := T+1 to C do        -- Loop from point of interruption
20       Parts[i-P] := Parts[i];   -- Scooch 'em up
21     end;
22     C := C - P;                 -- Reduce count by number leaving

23
24                 /* Move Particles */
25     Temp := Temp@south;         -- Send particles N
26     P := P@south;               -- Send count of arrived particles

27
28                 /* Incorporate particles */
29     for i := 1 to P do
30       Parts[C+i] := Temp[i];    -- Add to list, or no-op if none
31     end;
32     C := C + P;                 -- If particle arrived, bump count
33   end;
```

Figure 9.5
Batched particle solution for pushing points north

```
  mid: float;
count: integer;
```

Notice that the values are chosen to be of floating-point type, but other types can be handled simply by changing declarations.

The strategy is to begin with an interval that spans the whole set of numbers,

```
lo := min<< A;
hi := max<< A;
```

and then to shrink it iteratively

```
[R] while hi != lo do
      mid := (hi - lo)/2;          -- Figure midpoint
      M := A < (lo + mid);         -- Which items are smaller
      count := +<< M;              -- How many are there
      if count < ceil(n/2)         -- Is median in upper half?
         then
            [" without M] lo := min<< A; -- Yes, move lo up
         else
            [" with M] hi := max<< A;    -- No, move hi down
      end;
    end;
```

The computation proceeds as follows. If the values between lo and hi inclusive are the same, then that value is the median value. Otherwise, the midpoint between the two endpoints is determined, and a mask, M, is computed with a 1 set for each element less than the midpoint. The total count of these elements is then computed. If count is less than $n/2$, then the median element must be in the half larger than mid, and lo should be adjusted up. Otherwise, hi should be adjusted down.

The adjustment masks the R region to consider the indices of only a subset of the elements. (Recall that ditto ["] is synonymous with "the current region.") When the mask employs the without operator, the elements larger than or equal to the midpoint (corresponding to zeroes of M) are considered, and the minimum of these elements becomes the new lo endpoint. Symmetrically, when the mask employs the with operator, the elements smaller than the midpoint (corresponding to ones) are considered, and the maximum of these becomes the new hi endpoint. The iteration continues until the interval collapses.

It is instructive to consider the convergence of the algorithm. Consider first the case when A has Index1 as its value. The snapshot of the relevant program variables (prior to the if-statement) of each iteration is shown. (The values do not have to be in order to produce this result, of course, but order makes the logic somewhat easier to follow.)

Array A	lo	hi	mid	Array M	count
1 2 3 4 5 6 7 8 9	1	9	4	1 1 1 1 0 0 0 0 0	4
	5	9	2	1 1 1 1 1 1 0 0 0	6
	5	6	0.5	1 1 1 1 1 0 0 0 0	5
	5	5			

The three iteration convergence illustrated is not dependent on the value of n. A moment's thought indicates that any odd length sequence of consecutive integers converges in three steps, because the first iteration will throw out all elements below the median, the second will purge those above the median+1, and the last will shrink this two element interval to a single element. (An array of identical values doesn't iterate.) In general, the algorithm uses a Fibonacci search to push the end points toward the median.

Readers who are conversant with ZPL's WYSIWYG performance model will notice the repeated use of reduction operations. Though efficiently implemented, reduction is a global operation requiring communication and it is generally a good principle to reduce its use when possible. In the median program, as with many computations, reduction is essential.

Random Number Generation

Computers do not generate truly random numbers, of course, though sometimes a buggy program will seem to the frustrated programmer to be doing so. Rather, they generate pseudo-random numbers—a finite sequence of dependent numbers that over the sequence appears to have the statistical properties of random quantities. The generation of pseudo-random numbers is a deep and interesting topic in computer science, and the reader is warned that generating pseudo-random numbers by "random" methods doesn't work [Knuth 69]. Consequently, since random numbers are widely used in scientific computations, they are briefly considered here.

A reliable technique for generating high quality pseudo-random numbers on contemporary machines having 32-bit integer arithmetic is the Learmonth-Lewis prime-modulus multiplicative congruential generator [Learmonth & Lewis 1974],

$$r_n = 16807 r_{n-1} \bmod (2^{31}-1)$$

where r_0, called the *seed*, is given initially. The sequence sweeps through the full range of positive integers for 32-bit twos complement representation, $\{1, \ldots, 2^{31}-2\}$, two billion numbers in all, before repeating. (Zero could not be generated, of course, since to do so would kill the sequence.)

The Learmonth-Lewis generator can be converted into a scalar ZPL function directly. It is convenient to define a constant for the modulus, so that it need not be continually recomputed,

```
constant llmodulus : uinteger = 2147483647;
                                         -- Set modulus to 2^31 - 1
          multiplier: uinteger = 16807;  -- Set multiplier to 7^5
          recipmod  : double   = 4.6566128752457969E-10;
                                         -- Reciprocal of modulus
```

as well as the multiplier and the reciprocal of the modulus. Also, declare

```
var seed : uinteger;
```

and initialize it

```
seed = 377003613;      -- Set seed
```

with some arbitrary value. This value can be changed for production runs, say with the time of day. Specifying a fixed initial value assures that debugging runs are repeatable.

The scalar function

```
procedure llrand(var rsequence: uinteger) : uinteger;
/*    Learmonth-Lewis prime modulus random number generator
                    for 32-bit arithmetic                    */
var rhi, rmlo, fhi : uinteger;
begin
    rhi := bsr(rsequence, 16);
    rmlo:= (bsr(bsl(rsequence, 16), 16) * multiplier;
    fhi := rhi * multiplier + bsr(rmlo, 16);
    rsequence := (bsr(bsl(rmlo, 16), 16)
                + bsr(bsl(fhi, 17), 1)) + bsr(fhi, 15);
    if rsequence >= llmodulus
       then rsequence -= llmodulus;
    end;
    return rsequence;
end;
```

takes r_{n-1} in as a var parameter, i.e., rsequence is by-reference, and produces r_n. The involved right and left shifting is designed to assure that the large, intermediate products do not cause overflow.

   This function is invoked with the call

```
...  llrand(seed)  ...
```

whenever a random (scalar) integer value is needed. If random floating point numbers are desired, then changing the procedure's return type to double and changing the next to last line to

```
return rsequence * recipmod;
```

produces uniformly distributed random floating point numbers over $(0,1)$.

   The llrand procedure can be tested by beginning with the previously initialized seed and comparing with the following test sequence, which has elements separated by 100,000 llrand calls:

$$r_0 \qquad = 377,003,613$$
$$r_{100,000} = 648,473,574$$
$$r_{200,000} = 1,396,717,869$$
$$r_{300,000} = 2,027,350,275$$
$$r_{400,000} = 1,356,162,430$$

An important point to notice is that because seed is a scalar, ZPL will replicate its value on every processor, as explained in chapter 8. Accordingly, when llrand is called, every processor will produce the same pseudo-random scalar value. This can be used like all other scalars in ZPL.

   For cases where an array, A, is to be initialized to random values, the code

```
      /*   Set A to a random initial value          */
         for i := 1 to n do
            for j := 1 to m do
[i,j]          A := llrand(seed);                      (*)
            end;
      end;
```

performs the operations such that the sequence $r_1, r_2, \ldots$ is assigned to elements of A in row-major order.

   The loops initialize the array one position at a time, and since this is a sequence, the computation is sequential. That is, by using a single point region within the loops, all r_{mn}

elements are swept through one at a time. Notice that each processor will execute this loop ensuring that all processors have the same `seed` value upon completion. The process is fast, and is likely to contribute negligibly to the overall execution time of any serious computation, so alternative initializations are not considered.

A final cautionary note about arrays of random numbers. The `llrand` procedure given above is scalar, and could be promoted to compute over an array, just like any scalar procedure. Array sequences of random numbers could be generated by promoting `llrand` to apply to an array `Seed`, provided it is initialized properly. *The initialization (*) above is not appropriate for this application.* This is because the kth element in the sequence of $Seed_{ij+1}$ is the $k+1^{st}$ element of the sequence for $Seed_{ij}$. That is, the elements are correlated. Thus, the previous initialization is ideal for single uses such as initialization, but not for array sequences of random numbers.

References

Donald E. Knuth, 1969, *The Art of Computer Programming, Vol. 2, Seminumerical Algorithms,* Addison-Wesley.

G. P. Learmonth and P. A. W. Lewis, 1974, "Statistical tests of some widely used and recently proposed uniform random number generators," *Proceedings of the 7th Conference on Computer Science and Statistical Interface.*

10 ZPL and Future Parallel Programming

ZPL has introduced a series of new, high level programming concepts to simplify the task of parallel computing, and in addition, simplified known techniques such as array manipulation. Perhaps the most significant contribution is the WYSIWYG performance estimation capability. Throughout the language, regions are key to making clean, easy-to-use programming facilities. What more could be done? Plenty.

On the horizon is Advanced ZPL, a superset of ZPL—all ZPL programs are legal A-ZPL programs—in which there are more sophisticated data structuring facilities, more powerful programming facilities, e.g., pipelining, and more tightly integrated tools. Advanced ZPL will elevate programming to a higher level of abstraction subject to the conditions that ZPL's high performance and portability be maintained.

ZPL provides access to a set of built-in facilities to simplify programming. The fundamental constants and standard scientific functions come from the C language's `math.h` library on the host computer.

Fundamental Constants

The following double precision floating point constants are provided:

Name	Meaning	Decimal Value
m_e	e	2.7182818284590452354
m_log2e	$\log_2 e$	1.4426950408889634074
m_log10e	$\log_{10} e$	0.43429448190325182765
m_ln2	$\log_e 2$	0.69314718055994530942
m_ln10	$\log_e 10$	2.30258509299404568402
m_pi	π	3.14159265358979323846
m_pi_2	$\pi/2$	1.57079632679489661923
m_pi_4	$\pi/4$	0.78539816339744830962
m_1_pi	$1/\pi$	0.31830988618379067154
m_2_pi	$2/\pi$	0.63661977236758134308
m_2_sqrtpi	$2/\sqrt{\pi}$	1.12837916709551257390
m_sqrt2	$\sqrt{2}$	1.41421356237309504880
m_sqrt_2	$1/\sqrt{2}$	0.70710678118654752440

Scientific Functions

The following standard scientific functions are provided in multiple forms, one generic form and other type-specific forms. Use of the generic function will result in the compiler generating a call to the proper type-specific library routine matching the argument type or higher argument type when there are two arguments.

Name	Meaning
abs(x)	Absolute value of x
acos(x)	Arc cosine of x
asine(x)	Arc sine of x
atan(x)	Arc tangent of x
atan2(x,y)	Arc tan of x/y
ceil(x)	Least integer not less than x
cos(x)	Cosine
cosh(x)	Hyperbolic cosine
cube(x)	x^3
exp(x)	e^x
floor(x)	Greatest integer not greater than x
fmod(x,y)	Floating point remainder of x/y
ldexp(x,y)	$x2^y$
log(x)	Logarithm to base e of x
log2(x)	Logarithm to base 2 of x
log10(x)	Logarithm to base 10 of x
pow(x,y)	x^y
sin(x)	Sine of x
sinh(x)	Hyperbolic sine of x
sqrt(x)	Squareroot of x
tan(x)	Tangent of x
tanh(x)	Hyperbolic tangent of x
trunc(x)	Truncate x to a whole number

Type-specific standard functions can be called explicitly. To construct the name of a type-specific standard function, append the type designation letter(s) to the generic function name, precision first. The type designation letters are

f = single precision floating point,

d = double precision floating point,

q = quad precision floating point,

c = complex

For example, `sin(x)` calls the sine function matching the type of `x`; `sinf(x)` is the single precision sine function, `sind(x)` is the double precision sine, `sinq(x)` is the quad precision sine when quad precision is available, and `sinfc(x)`, `sindc(x)` and `sinqc(x)` are the corresponding complex calls. Arguments not matching the type of type-specific standard function are converted.

Timers

Two timing functions are provided based on the native timer of the host computer. Timing granularity varies widely, and is not always very fine. Accordingly, timing very small sections of program can be inaccurate.

`ResetTimer()`   Resets the timer to zero and returns a double precision floating point number that is the number of seconds since the last call to `ResetTimer()`.

`CheckTimer()`   Returns a double precision floating point number that is the number of seconds since the last call to `ResetTimer()`.

Check your installation's documentation for details.

Index